# *f*INANCING
# GRADUATE
# SCHOOL

## PATRICIA McWADE

HOW TO GET THE

MONEY FOR YOUR

MASTER'S

OR PH.D.

Peterson's
Princeton, New Jersey

Visit Peterson's at http://www.petersons.com

**Library of Congress Cataloging-in-Publication Data**

McWade Patricia.
    Financing graduate school : how to get the money you need for your graduate school education / Patricia McWade. p. cm.
    Includes bibliographical references and index.
    ISBN 1-56079-638-3
    1. Student aid—United States. 2. Universities and colleges—United States—Graduate work—Case studies. 3. Federal aid to higher education—United States.
I Title.
LB2337.4.M34    1996 IN PROCESS
378.3'3'0973—dc20

96-31265
CIP

Editorial direction by Carol Hupping
Editing by Bart Astor
Production supervision by Bernadette Boylan
Composition by Linda Williams
Creative direction by Linda Huber
Interior design by Cynthia Boone

# Contents

# $\mathcal{P}$reface

This book is a revised version of the book I wrote for Peterson's in 1993. Its purpose is to answer the most frequently asked questions that students and those who advise them have about funding sources at the graduate level.

My experience in graduate financing aid comes from my years at the Harvard Graduate School of Arts and Sciences and at Georgetown University. The book is, therefore, geared to graduate study in master's and Ph.D. programs and does not contain as much information about professional schools such as law, medicine, and business. Fortunately, these are areas where other books are available. I suggest you consult the professional school "experts" for the latest in law, medical, and business school financial aid.

That said, I hope that you find the information in this book helpful. Perhaps it will lead you to sources of support you may not have thought to consider. I hope it will also save you time and work in the often time-consuming and tedious—but frequently rewarding—task of finding money for graduate school.

# Acknowledgments

A very special thank you goes to Richard Galentino and Jennifer Raley, my student assistants at Georgetown. Their research and excellent suggestions make the revised edition an even better book than the original text.

# $\mathcal{I}$ntroduction

efore I begin discussing how to find and get money for graduate school, let me raise a few important basic questions you should ask yourself first. You'll be investing a lot of time and money in graduate school, so your decisions about where and when to go or even whether to go at all, should be well thought out. You should also take into consideration the anticipated return on your investment in enrolling in graduate school.

## WILL A GRADUATE DEGREE MAKE A DIFFERENCE IN YOUR EARNINGS?

Statistics show that those with advanced degrees earn more over their working lifetime than those with only a bachelor's degree.

"When I first received information on graduate programs, I was shocked at how much it was going to cost to get an M.A. in allied health," says Bernice Winters, a registered nurse who waited three years after getting her B.A. to enroll in a master's program. "But then I realized how much in salary I was losing each year because I didn't have one. Without a graduate degree, the most I could make—even with twenty years' experience—was $33,000. With an M.A. I would jump instantly from my present salary of $25,000 to $29,000. And the ceiling for someone after twenty years in my job was $47,000, over 40 percent more than the maximum without a master's degree. All of which didn't even take into account the ease with which I could switch to both a higher level and a higher paying position anytime I chose. When I looked at the whole thing through *those* glasses, the decision literally made itself."

Many factors affect your salary, including your field of work, the size of the company in which you're employed, and the area of the country in which you live. Comparative starting salaries for workers with bachelor's degrees and those with advanced degrees are shown in the chart on page 2.

## Comparative Starting Salaries

| Field | Degree | Annual Gross Salary |
| --- | --- | --- |
| Accountant | Bachelor's | $28,000 |
| | Master's | over $30,000 |
| Chemist | Bachelor's | $24,000 |
| | Master's | $32,000 |
| | Ph.D. | $48,000 |
| Engineer | Bachelor's | $34,000 |
| | Master's | $39,200 |
| | Ph.D. | $54,400 |
| Mathematician | Bachelor's | $28,400 |
| | Master's | $33,600 |
| | Ph.D. | $41,000 |
| Teacher | Bachelor's | $23,200 * |
| | Master's | $26,100 * |
| Social Worker | Bachelor's | $20,000 |
| | Master's | $30,000 |
| Statistical Analyst | Bachelor's | $26,800 * |
| | Master's | $31,400 * |
| Nurse | Bachelor's | $22,500 * |
| | Master's | $27,300 * |

* Adapted from the Bureau of Labor Statistics Population Survey.

Source: Occupational Outlook Handbook, 1994–95 edition, U.S. Department of Labor Bureau of Labor Statistics, May 1994.

Overall, the *Education Daily* estimates the median wage and salary earnings for those with a bachelor's degree to be $32,629. For those with a master's degree, however, the figure jumps to $40,368. The chart on page 3 demonstrates the differences in salary for each level of education. "There is no job we know of where there is not a significant jump in wages when a person goes on for education after the bachelor's," says Leo Rydzewski, an economist with the Washington-based Bureau of Labor Statistics. In fact, he points out, of the ten jobs considered to be among the best-paying options for women, eight require advanced degrees.

## Mean Annual Earnings by Level of Education, 1992

| | |
|---|---|
| Professional Degree | $74,560 |
| Doctorate | 54,904 |
| Master's Degree | 40,368 |
| Bachelor's Degree | 32,629 |
| Associate Degree | 24,398 |
| Some College, No Degree | 19,666 |
| High School Diploma | 18,737 |
| No High School Diploma | 12,809 |

Source: *Education Daily,* November 29, 1994.

# SHOULD YOU GO PART TIME OR FULL TIME?

According to Peter Syverson, Vice President for Research and Information Services for the Council of Graduate Schools, most graduate students—over 60 percent of those enrolled—attend part time. "The reason," he says, "is that many continue to keep the jobs they already have. Half are over thirty, and their career choices are pretty much made. The main reason they have for going back to school is to enhance their job skills so that they can move up in their present positions." In general, where the master's degree predominates, such as business and education, most students attend part-time. In the disciplines in which the doctorate is the focal degree, most students attend full time. One key exception to this rule is engineering where a master's degree is generally considered the professional terminal degree, but the majority of students are enrolled full time.

Take Jeff Lewis, for example. For him, attending full time wasn't a choice. "I originally wanted to go part time," says Lewis, who is now a Ph.D. biochemist with a St. Louis company specializing in agricultural technology. "The problem was the courses weren't available either in the evenings or on weekends. At first, I thought, 'That's it, I can't go at all.' Besides everything else, my wife and I had two small children. But then I did some creative thinking about our finances and the value of a job that really wasn't going anywhere anyway. My wife went back to her law practice, and we hired someone to help us with child care. The next four years were rough, but we got through them."

3

In general, where the master's degree predominates, such as business and education, most students attend part time. In the disciplines in which the doctorate is the focal degree, most students attend full time. One key exception to this rule is engineering where a master's degree is generally considered the professional terminal degree, but the majority of students are enrolled full time.

The chart that follows gives the breakdown of full- and part-time students per discipline for 1993, the most current period for which such information is available.

## Graduate Enrollment by Field, Fall 1994

| Major Field | Full Time | Part Time |
|---|---|---|
| **Total** | 563,899—49% | 588,835—51% |
| Biological Sciences* | 46,469—75% | 15,713—25% |
| Business | 64,937—40% | 98,521—60% |
| Education | 73,155—31% | 163,874—69% |
| Engineering | 61,295—59% | 41,837—41% |
| Health Sciences | 40,050—53% | 35,238—47% |
| Humanities & Arts | 65,297—64% | 36,636—36% |
| Physical Sciences | 62,325—65% | 33,796—35% |
| Public Administration and Services | 23,824—55% | 19,507—45% |
| Social Sciences | 65,088—63% | 38,518—37% |
| Other Fields** | 42,454—45% | 50,889—55% |

* "Biological sciences" includes agriculture. ** The category "other fields" includes architecture, communications, home economics, library sciences, and religion.

Source: CGS/GRE Survey of Graduate Enrollment.

# 10 QUESTIONS TO ASK YOURSELF

If you're having a particularly hard time deciding whether to go full or part time, the following ten questions might help you make up your mind:

    1. Are there any sources of financial aid that will be available to me only if I attend full time?

2. Will I be able to make as many professional contacts if I only go part time; especially given that most academic departments are, for all intents and purposes, closed during off-hours?
3. Will the courses I need be available when I need them?
4. If I enroll in a certain program because of the availability of jobs in that field, will those jobs still be available when I graduate? How about if I go part time and it takes me two or three times as long to graduate?
5. If the program features "name" professors, do those professors teach only in the daytime?
6. Will I feel as involved in the field if I only take a few courses at a time?
7. Will I be *more* involved in the field if I'm working at the same time as taking course work in my area of study?
8. Are support services (libraries, administrative offices, registrars, counseling centers) open during off-hours?
9. How safe is it for me to travel to school in the evening?
10. What is the comparison between the amount of money I lose by going full time versus the increased amount of money I can earn when I've completed my degree?

With the advent of "distance learning," some of these questions may not matter. However, if you are considering graduate study, you should consider whether you want to actually participate in departmental activities unavailable via computer technology.

# DISTANCE LEARNING

Distance learning—gaining acdemic credit through computer, television, or other telecommunications media—is one of the fastest growing educational alternatives today and offers a unique solution to specific graduate school needs. For many students, these alternative programs are both cost- and time-effective. *Peterson's Guide to Distance Learning* (Peterson's, 1996) gives a comprehensive list of alternatives at both the undergraduate and graduate levels at more than 700 American and Canadian colleges and universities for the following:

- credit (and degree) for life experience learning, even if the learning took place long before you entered school
- credit (and degree) for independent study, whether or not you were enrolled in a school at the time

- credit (and degree) for work done on your home computer, linked to your school's computer, wherever in the world it may be

- credit (and degree) through the use of audio and videotaped courses that you can review at your convenience

In addition to *Virtual College* (Peterson's, 1996) is a quick guide to earning credits and degrees off campus. It provides information on program selection, equipment needed, transferring credits, financial aid, and what it's like to be in a virtual classroom. Two other books about distance learning are John Bear's *Guide to Earning College Degrees Nontraditionally* (Ten Speed Press, 1995) and *College Degrees You Can Earn From Your Home* by Judith Frey (Boulder, CO: Live Oak Publications, 1995).

# WHEN SHOULD YOU GO TO GRAD SCHOOL?

Should you go to graduate school right after undergraduate school or get a job first and go later? Here are the stories of two students who handled the timing of their graduate school education in very different ways.

Peter T. graduated in anthropology in the top tenth of his college class. When he was still in his junior year, he decided he wanted to go for graduate work at the University of Michigan. His ideal would have been to work a few years to pay off his student loans. But his undergraduate adviser told him he would have an impossible time getting into the program if he waited even a semester. "Anthropology is a research-oriented field," the adviser said. "If you wait, your academic knowledge and skill will be considered obsolete." Peter applied in January 1995. In June, he received his bachelor's and went directly into the graduate anthropology program. "Professors here have since told me I did the right thing," he says. "According to them, if I'd waited, I'd probably never have gotten in."

Janet W. majored in economics at Washington State University. As she contemplated graduate school, there was only one program that piqued her interest—the M.B.A. When she talked to her adviser, however, she was told that the average number of years M.B.A. applicants have been out of college has risen from two and a half to four. "It's becoming increasingly important for M.B.A. students to have some significant career experience," the adviser said.

Janet ignored the advice and applied to six programs—the University of Chicago Graduate School of Business, Dartmouth College's Amos Tuck School of Business Administration, Stanford University's School of Business, Harvard Business School, the MIT Sloan School of Management, and Northwestern University's J. L. Kellogg Graduate School of Business Management. Despite excellent undergraduate grades and a competitive score on the Graduate Management Admission Test, she was rejected by all of them. The reasons that she was given for her rejection by the schools were all basically the same: not enough practical experience.

From 1990 to 1994 Janet went to work for Shearson-Lehman, eventually getting promoted to a managerial position in the bonds department. It became clear to her at that point in her career that without additional education she could probably go no further. So Janet decided to try graduate school again. Not coincidentally, she applied to five of the original six programs. Plus, she added a new one for good luck, the University of Pennsylvania's Wharton School of Business, rated among the top five business schools in the country. All but Dartmouth accepted her. Janet is now in her last semester at Wharton.

Whether you go directly to graduate school from undergraduate study depends in large part on the field you choose to pursue. Those studying for the Ph.D. in chemistry, for example, will probably want to go on directly, given that they need recent letters from academics to successfully compete for a place. For those considering a graduate degree in environmental studies, however, the school may strongly recommend you work a few years to gain some practical experience.

Either way, it is a good idea to check with the program of your choice well in advance of the application process. It's also suggested that you talk to people working in the field—ask what they did, whether they went directly to graduate school or if they took a few years off to work and gain some experience, and what they recommend.

# IS IT NECESSARY TO GO TO GRADUATE SCHOOL?

Another factor that should affect your decision to go to graduate school is the relative demand for professionals in the career. The chart on the next page from the National Association of Colleges and Employers shows which careers are in high demand and which are not.

# DEMAND EXPECTED TO EXCEED SUPPLY

- Adult education teachers
- Chiropractors
- Computer scientists and systems analysts
- Construction and building inspectors
- Cost estimators
- Counselors
- Engineering, science, and data processing managers
- Funeral directors
- Health services managers
- Human services workers
- Inspectors and compliance officers, except construction
- Loan officers and counselors
- Metallurgical, ceramic, and materials engineers
- Occupational therapists
- Physician assistants
- Physicians
- Podiatrists
- Property and real estate managers
- Recreational therapists
- Registered nurses
- Respiratory therapists
- Restaurant and food service managers
- Roman Catholic priests
- School teachers—secondary and special education
- Speech language pathologists and audiologists
- Veterinarians

# DEMAND EXPECTED TO ABOUT EQUAL SUPPLY

- Accountants and auditors
- Agricultural scientists
- Chemical engineers
- Chemists
- Civil engineers
- College and university faculty
- Dietitians and nutritionists
- Economists and marketing research analysts
- Electrical and electronics engineers
- Employment interviewers
- Geologists and geophysicists
- Hotel managers and assistants
- Industrial engineers
- Industrial production managers
- Landscape architects
- Mechanical engineers
- Meteorologists
- Mining engineers
- Nuclear engineers
- Optometrists
- Petroleum engineers
- Rabbis
- Retail managers
- School teachers—kindergarten and elementary
- Social scientists and urban planners
- Social workers
- Sociologists
- Underwriters
- Urban and regional planners
- Writers and editors

# SUPPLY EXPECTED TO EXCEED DEMAND

- Actuaries
- Administrative services managers
- Aerospace engineers
- Architects
- Archivists and curators
- Biological and medical scientists
- Budget analysts
- Dentists
- Designers
- Education administrators
- Financial managers
- Foresters and conservation scientists
- Lawyers and judges
- Librarians
- Management analysts and consultants
- Marketing, advertising, and public relations managers
- Mathematicians
- Personnel, training, and labor relations specialists and managers

- Photographers and camera operators
- Protestant ministers
- Psychologists
- Public relations specialists
- Purchasers and buyers
- Radio and television announcers and news-casters

- Recreation workers
- Reporters and correspondents
- Statisticians
- Surveyors
- Visual artists

Source: "The 1992-2005 Job Outlook in Brief," Bureau of Labor Statistics, *Occupational Outlook Quarterly*/Spring 1994.

# HOW IMPORTANT IS A "NAME" SCHOOL?

A school's prestige and the career successes of its graduates go hand in hand. But which came first? Is Yale a name school because its graduates consistently rise to the top of their professions, or do they wind up there because they graduated from Yale? There's no question that corporate recruiters tend to do most of their interviews at the top twenty M.B.A. programs, law firms at the top twenty law schools, and residency and intern programs at the top twenty medical schools. The graduates from these top schools get the plum jobs, which then feeds the school's reputation.

In the case of engineering and science programs, the more prestigious schools have more money for top faculty and the latest in sophisticated lab equipment. The result, again, is that employers and research institutions tend to limit their recruiting to the top twenty schools.

Therefore, if you have an opportunity to attend one of the top schools, you will increase your chances of having future career success. However, another point to consider is the relative ease with which you will be able to attain an impressive academic record at one of the less-than-top twenty schools. In one situation, an undergraduate who spent four years on her state college's Dean's List complained of Harvard's graduate school grading: "It's almost impossible to get an A here. If I'd gone to Central Connecticut State, I'd be in the top percentile of my class. Here, I'm lucky to make the top half."

# WHAT ABOUT JOB PLACEMENT?

Many students go through their graduate programs concerned about their ability to get a job in their chosen fields after completing their programs of study. If this sounds like you, you should ask about the school's job placement rate before you decide to enroll. Be sure you also check with former graduates or prospective employers, not just the school. And don't be vague about it. To get a clear answer you need to ask pointed questions. But be sure you also find out the overall placement rate of the profession in general when comparing a particular school's rate. Keep in mind that if a school advertises its job placement rates, it must also publish the most recent available data about employment statistics, graduation statistics, and any other information to back up its claims. This information should be available at, or ideally before, the time you apply for admission to the school.

# CAN YOU AFFORD TO GO TO GRADUATE SCHOOL?

One of the major questions facing most people about to enter a graduate program is "How can I pay for it?" If you have doubts about your ability to afford graduate school, it could be because you have heard one or more of the common myths about getting financial aid—myths that prevent many people from taking full advantage of everything that's available to them. Some of these myths are:

- Financial aid is just for poor people.

- Financial aid is mainly for minorities.

- Financial aid is just for smart people.

- Loans are not financial aid.

- If I have a job, I'm not eligible for financial aid.

- If I apply for aid, it will affect whether or not I'm admitted.

## THE COST OF ATTENDANCE

Aid *is* available for graduate study, and it's a good thing, because graduate school can be expensive. It often costs more than undergraduate school, and some programs, particularly law and medicine, cost *considerably* more than undergraduate programs. To compound your problem of paying for it, there's only a limited amount of government aid available. And if that weren't enough, many graduate programs require such a heavy academic load that it becomes difficult, if not impossible, to hold a job while attending school. To give you an idea of

**11**

just how much it costs at the graduate level, the following chart shows the range of annual tuition charges at various schools across the country.

### Range of Annual Tuition and Fees Nationwide

|  | Private Institutions | Public Institutions |
|---|---|---|
| Business School | Georgetown $19,600 | U. of Massachusetts $4,232 (resident) $8,570 (out-of-state) |
| Engineering | Carnegie Mellon $18,520 | UC Berkeley $4,650 (resident) $12,349 (out-of-state) |
| Liberal Arts, M.A. | Wesleyan $19,903 | U. of Michigan $8.409 (resident) $16,995 (out-of-state) |

Note: The number of years usually required to earn a graduate degree is: M.D., 4; LL.B. or J.D., 3; M.B.A., 2; M.A. or M.S., 1 to 2; Ph.D., 2 to 3 years of course work, plus a dissertation and/or a medical internship that can take an additional 2 to 5 years (during this time tuition is often reduced).

The cost of attending graduate school for one academic year includes not only the direct expenses such as tuition, fees, and books, but also your living expenses. This total is what is known as your *cost of attendance*, and it is the basis on which need-based financial aid awards are determined.

# STANDARD STUDENT BUDGETS

Most schools divide costs into categories and use standard student budgets to determine eligibility for need-based financial aid. Naturally, there are variations from one student's budget to another's. Students who attend graduate school in New York City, for example, will pay much more in rent than a student in Jackson, Mississippi, and standard student budgets reflect these differences. But standard budgets don't necessarily reflect your individual family's circumstances. So, if you have special expenses—a constant flow of medical bills or unusually high traveling expenses, for example—you should make a point of bringing those circumstances to the attention of a financial aid counselor so that they can be included in your budget.

The elements and amounts used to calculate the cost of attendance are determined by the school. The following are generally considered allowable expenses for purposes of awarding need-based aid:

### Direct expenses:

*Tuition*: the fixed tuition charged to students by the school.

*Required fees*: includes only student fees required of all students carrying the same workload. If a fee is optional, such as a student activity fee, it may be included in the cost at the discretion of the institution. Fees for rental or purchase of equipment, materials, or supplies must be required of *all* students in the same course of study in order to be included in the student's budget.

*Books and supplies*: an amount determined by each institution, generally an average cost that takes into account textbooks and supplies. The cost of a computer, word processor, or software program can only be included if the school requires that *all* students in a particular program purchase any of these items.

### Indirect expenses:

*Living expenses*: an allowance for room and board costs, whether in school housing or your own apartment or house. Generally, an average reasonable budget is used, and many schools conduct surveys to determine the actual living costs in the area. Under the regulations governing federal financial aid programs, only the student's expenses can be included. If you have a spouse or dependent children, their expenses are taken into account in the need analysis formula to determine the family contribution.

*Transportation*: includes the cost of travel between the student's residence and the school plus any travel costs required to complete a course of study. Each school has its own policy regarding travel allowances for students traveling longer distances home for brief visits. Some schools build in a budget item for travel that covers the cost of two or more round-trip fares between the school and the student's home city.

*Personal expenses*: the average allowance for such items as clothing, laundry, grooming aids, insurance, and recreation.

*Child care:* an allowance for reasonable expenses incurred for dependent care.

*Summer costs*: standard budgets take into account the actual period of enrollment, which is generally only the nine-month academic year. However, a school may, at its discretion, include costs associated with summer enrollment, using a twelve-month budget. This includes both the direct and indirect expenses previously listed.

*Loan-origination and insurance fees*: many loan programs, both federal and private, charge a fee for borrowing money. Lenders generally deduct origination and insurance fees from the proceeds of the loan. As a result, the amount you actually receive is less than the amount you borrow. Many graduate schools either take these fees into account in setting student budgets, or provide enough money in the financial aid package to cover the additional costs.

*Miscellaneous add-ons*: based on extenuating circumstances, the financial aid office may take into account other expenses or increase the individual elements used in the standard budgets. These add-ons must be well-documented and are made on a case-by-case basis.

*Expenses due to a disability*: an allowance determined by the school for expenses relating to a disability, including any special services, transportation, equipment, and supplies.

## Direct and Indirect Expenses for Awarding Need-Based Financial Aid

| Direct Expenses | Indirect Expenses |
|---|---|
| Tuition | Living expenses |
| Required fees | Personal expenses |
| Transportation | Child care |
| Books and supplies | Summer costs |
| Loan origination and insurance fees | Miscellaneous add-ons |
| Disabled student expenses | |

### Need Formula

Cost of Attendance – Student Contribution = Financial Need

# THE IMPORTANCE OF FINANCIAL PLANNING

"I've been going to school now for eighteen years and am about to begin a doctoral program that won't be completed for another six," says Jean Shaver, a civil engineer in Albuquerque, New Mexico. "Since high school, I've been paying for my education myself, and I have to tell you, figuring out how to get the money has consistently been one of my major concerns. Yet, there's never been a time when any teacher, in any course, has even hinted at the importance of financial planning. No wonder so many students start their careers saddled with a debt burden they won't get out from under until they're middle-aged!"

Regardless of what economic level you come from, or whether or not your parents have always picked up the tab for your education, sound financial planning is one of the absolute essentials for a successful and stress-minimized lifestyle. But what does financial planning mean? Initially, it means having thorough mastery of the following three basic principles:

1. thinking ahead

2. establishing a budget that is realistic and flexible enough to take into account a variety of possible changes in your financial situation

3. managing your debts

# THINKING AHEAD

For those considering graduate school, thinking ahead requires that you consider such items as:

- the loss of income you may experience while you're in graduate school

- income projections for the duration of your graduate education, as well as for the ten to twenty years after you get your degree

- inflation rates—actual and projected

- cash flow—actual and projected

- spouse or family income and any anticipated changes that may take place during the next five years

- loss of income that may result from pregnancy, disability, or unintentional periods of unemployment

The cornerstone of thinking ahead is having an understanding of the overall nature of financial planning—the step-by-step process that ensures that you'll be able to do what you want (in this case, go to graduate school) without becoming entangled in an unmanageable debt burden that will be with you for the next twenty years. There are six steps to the thinking ahead process. They are:

1. **Setting Your Goals.** Decide what you want to study, where you want to study, whether you will go full time or part time, whether you will work to support all or some of your education, and what might be your appropriate level of debt.

2. **Taking Inventory.** Collect all your financial information (and that of any member of your family who will be contributing to the cost of your education) to determine what assets you have. Included under assets are cash, bank accounts, stocks and bonds, real estate, and business and personal property. Next, subtract your liabilities—any monies owed on the assets listed above as well as credit card debt and loans. The final number you get when you finish the subtraction is your net worth.

3. **Doing an Analysis.** By combining your net worth from step two with a realistic budget you can arrive at a rough evaluation of how much money you'll need to pay for your graduate education.

4. **Designing a Financial Plan.** Using the analysis you just finished, create a plan of action that will provide you with the necessary funds. First, determine how much you plan to earn, how much you think you might receive in grants, and how much you plan to borrow (taking into consideration that you might not get *any* grant money). Next, compare loan rates to figure out which plans offer the most attractive terms (information on loans is provided in Chapters 3 and 4). Finally, take into consideration both inflation rates and any possible life changes that could affect your overall financial situation.

5. **Implementing Your Plan.** Here is where you adjust your lifestyle to begin living within the budget established in step three, send out résumés for whatever amount of work you decided you could handle as part of step four, and gather the necessary forms to apply for the grants and loans.

6. **Reviewing Your Plan.** The review process requires that you measure the progress of your financial plan, and that you make adjustments to account for such things as increases in salary (which could allow you to decrease the amount of your loans), or any other changes in goals or circumstances. You may, for example, decide to do an internship in another state instead of near home, a change in circumstance that would affect the personal cost-of-living part of your budget.

# FINANCIAL PLANNING STARTS WITH A BUDGET

"I know that most people are familiar with financial planning to help them manage their lives," says Ted Gershman, a second-year law student at the University of North Carolina. "But it was new to me and I've had to learn very quickly."

Last year Ted took out a loan to help him get through law school. The strategy he used to decide on the amount he would borrow was to make a quick mental calculation of how much he might need for tuition, books, and the cost of traveling to and from the university. What he neglected to plan for, however, were such things as the rent increase every year, the income he lost as a result of switching from full time to part time work so that he could devote more time to his classwork, and some unexpected costs, such as having to put a new transmission in his car. As a result, Ted was over $15,000 short of the amount he needed to continue his education.

"When I finally realized I was in over my head," explained Ted, "I went to see my financial aid counselor. She showed me how to figure out what I need both now and long term—in other words, she showed me how to do a budget. As she explained the ins and outs of itemizing my financial needs, I couldn't help thinking how I wish I'd learned this strategy a long time ago."

A graduate student financial plan requires no knowledge of high finance—just a knowledge of opportunities and a willingness to put in the time to determine a realistic assessment of your needs versus your resources. To say, "I'll figure it out when the time comes," or "If I wind up with too much debt, I'll get an extra job, much as I hate the idea," is being neither realistic nor fair to yourself. Generally, there *is* a way to get the money you need. All it requires is patience and a commitment to working out your plan.

## Schools' "Standard" Budgets

As we saw in Ted's case, one of the most important components of a good financial plan is the budget. The budget must include all of the expenses you'll face for the year. The chart on pages 19–20 contains a list of expenses and sources of income a "typical" graduate student has over a one-year period. You can use this list to generate your own budget. There is also space for you to fill in the school-related costs. Since graduate schools are required to publish their "standard" budgets, this information is available in the graduate school's consumer information booklets.

When creating your budget and comparing the cost of different schools, be certain you clarify whether the school is using a nine- or twelve-month "standard" budget (some even use ten-month budgets). The budget each school uses is tied to the length of the period of enrollment; each school counts only the months of the year during which you will be a student.

Keep in mind that standard budgets may be lower than you think they should be for your particular needs. If this is the case, be sure to have a discussion with the financial aid counselor at the schools where you intend to apply to see if they are willing to adjust the standard budget to include your additional expenses.

While federal financial aid programs require standard budgets, financial aid counselors can adjust the standard budget of a student if circumstances warrant a change. When requesting a budget adjustment, however, one word of caution: do not approach the financial aid counselor with an exorbitant budget that does not reflect the modest lifestyle expected of a graduate student. Most aid counselors will listen and are understanding if you have unusual financial needs that exceed the standard budget. But they won't be very receptive if you present them with a cost-of-living budget that exceeds their own living expense budget. Use good judgment in these situations. Each person's financial needs are different; but as a rule, the lifestyle of a graduate student receiving financial aid should not be extravagant. Remember, much of the money you receive will be taxpayer's money. Taxpayers do not generally like the idea of funding an extravagant lifestyle.

When doing a budget, the best strategy is to do it twice—once using a best-case scenario and again, using a worst-case scenario. That way you eliminate the possibility of being surprised by having either overestimated or underestimated. The actual amount you'll wind up using will be probably be somewhere in between.

## Typical Expenses and Income of a Graduate Student

| Personal Costs | Month | Year |
|---|---|---|
| Housing | _____ | _____ |
| Food | _____ | _____ |
| Utilities | _____ | _____ |
| Telephone | _____ | _____ |
| Clothing | _____ | _____ |
| Laundry/dry cleaning | _____ | _____ |
| Entertainment | _____ | _____ |
| Personal expenses | _____ | _____ |
| Transportation | _____ | _____ |
| Insurance | _____ | _____ |
| Medical expenses | _____ | _____ |
| Child care (if applicable) | _____ | _____ |
| Credit cards | _____ | _____ |
| Other indebtedness | _____ | _____ |
| Total | _____ | _____ |

## School-Related Costs: A Projection Based on Three Possible Choices

| Graduate Schools | 1._____ | 2._____ | 3._____ |
|---|---|---|---|
| Costs | | | |
| Tuition | _____ | _____ | _____ |
| Fees | _____ | _____ | _____ |
| Books and supplies | _____ | _____ | _____ |
| Travel | _____ | _____ | _____ |
| Other | _____ | _____ | _____ |
| | _____ | _____ | _____ |
| | _____ | _____ | _____ |
| | _____ | _____ | _____ |
| | _____ | _____ | _____ |
| | _____ | _____ | _____ |
| Total for one year | _____ | _____ | _____ |

Sources of Funds

| | | | |
|---|---|---|---|
| Savings | _____ | _____ | _____ |
| Earnings, one year | _____ | _____ | _____ |
| Parent's contribution | _____ | _____ | _____ |
| Spouse's contribution | _____ | _____ | _____ |
| Scholarships | _____ | _____ | _____ |
| Fellowships | _____ | _____ | _____ |
| Federal and state aid administered by school | _____ | _____ | _____ |
| Loans | _____ | _____ | _____ |
| Veteran's benefits | _____ | _____ | _____ |
| Social Security benefits | _____ | _____ | _____ |
| Stocks, bonds | _____ | _____ | _____ |
| Other resources | _____ | _____ | _____ |
| Total available | _____ | _____ | _____ |

## Questions You Should Answer as You Plan for the Financing of Your Education

You should answer the questions below as you plan to finance your education. Some of the questions are general and apply to any school you might attend, others are more specific—relating to the programs and procedures of each school you are considering. You should complete this exercise regardless of where you plan to enroll. Remember, the financing of your education will involve a partnership between you, your family, the school you attend, and your lender(s).

1. What should I be doing now to prepare for the financial cost of my graduate school education?

2. What can I do to minimize the cost of my education once I arrive on campus?

3. What financing option(s) do I have if I cannot pay the full cost of my education from my own resources and those of my family?

4. What is the purpose of financial aid programs and what questions should I be asking about the process?

5. What is the basic philosophy of the financial aid system?
6. What financial aid programs are available to me at each of the schools I am considering?
7. What is the financial aid process and how do I apply for financial assistance?
8. What is done with the information I provide?
9. What should I know about the loans I am offered?
10. What impact will these loans have on me after I complete my education?

Source: Sue Ledwell, formerly with University of Pennsylvania Graduate School, now at Access Group.

# DEVELOPING A SOUND BUDGET

So far, we've talked about the specifics of "standard" budgets. But what about the day-to-day expenses—the $4.87 you need for a new hairbrush? The $1.50 bus ride? "When it comes to handling my monthly loan payments, I'm fine," says Jack Scanlon, a master's student in the University of Chicago's School of Architecture. "It's the nickel-and-dime stuff that throws me off. I guess I'm spoiled by always having had a good job and, therefore, having more than enough money to cover my daily expenses. Now I'm on a tight budget, and I'm amazed at the small-potato things I have to watch out for. Last week, I had lunch at an inexpensive Chinese restaurant and almost didn't have enough money to pay the tab!"

The key to financial planning is establishing and then adhering to a workable budget, not just a standard budget. By planning your spending ahead of time and listing all your expected expenses and income for a given period, you can keep your problems to a minimum. This is especially important for students who live on a restricted budget and have very little savings.

When planning a budget for graduate school, it's especially important that you start as free of debt as you can. Chances are you won't have enough income while you're in school to pay off a lot of your current debts. So, if you can, pay off any debts *before* you start graduate school. (Of course this does not include most student loans since you will probably be able to defer student loan payments until you are in school.)

Second, if you have loans or financial obligations that are delinquent, be absolutely certain you make your payments before you apply for financial aid for graduate school. Most graduate students borrow to pay for their schooling and these loans require a good credit history. If you neglect to pay your consumer debts, they will appear on your credit report as bad debt. A bad credit history may make it all but impossible for you to receive an adequate amount of financial aid.

Another important aspect of budgeting is making your money last, that is, a good cash flow. Many students who pay for their education through a complex package of financial aid have difficulty with the fact that they get the bulk of their money at once. Some, for example, receive half of their Federal Stafford (or Direct) Student Loan and all their nonfederally guaranteed money within a short time of each other, often in the first semester. After paying tuition and school-related fees for the year, you could be left with less than $10,000 that has to last an entire semester. Budgeting for a lengthy period can be difficult for even the most experienced. For those unaccustomed to making lists and staying within budgets, the task can be mind-boggling.

Take a look at the sample budget on page 23. It's a nine-month budget for a single student living in an off-campus apartment during the 1996–97 academic year. Budgets like this one will vary from school to school, from city to city, and from situation to situation. Many factors will influence the amounts estimated in each of the spaces. An ideal course to follow is to review the anticipated expenses you'll face. This information is available through the school you plan to attend. Then, using figures that are realistic for your needs, compare the specific categories and amounts, like those listed in the chart following, with your own budget and your own anticipated resources. If your resources equal or exceed your expenses, you have a sound budget. If not, you'll have to find a way to make the numbers balance.

## Sample Student Budget
### Nine months, Single, No Dependents

| Fixed Expenses | Academic Year | Monthly |
|---|---|---|
| Rent or mortgage payment | $ 4,500 | $ 500 |
| Utilities (gas, electric, phone) | 540 | 60 |
| Total Fixed Expenses | $ 5,040 | $560 |

| Flexible Expenses | Academic Year | Monthly |
|---|---|---|
| Food and household goods | $ 2,700 | $ 300 |
| Books and supplies | 720 | 80 |
| Personal (including laundry cleaning, toiletries, etc.) | 1,800 | 200 |
| Transportation: gas/oil, car repairs, parking, license, insurance, etc. or carfare for public transportation | 700 | 80 |
| Travel (long distance) | 450 | 50 |
| Medical and dental expenses | 360 | 40 |
| Entertainment/recreation | 1,350 | 150 |
| Total Flexible Expenses | $ 8,100 | $ 900 |
| Total Expenses (Fixed + Flexible): | $13,140 | $1,460 |
| Plus Tuition and Fees | $_____ | $_____ |
| = Total Cost of Attendance | $_____ | $_____ |

# BALANCING YOUR EXPENSES WITH YOUR RESOURCES

"From a person who used to wing it with paying my bills, I've now turned into a compulsive list-maker," confesses Juan Melendez, a Ph.D. candidate in computer sciences. "The first thing I do on Monday is make a list of what I expect to spend that week. Then, I balance it against my monthly budget that is also balanced against a yearly budget. When you're a student, and you get six month's worth of money in one fell swoop, you have to make lists—there's no getting around it."

When your expenses are higher than your resources, you can either increase your income or reduce your expenditures. For most students, increasing income is a difficult proposition given the overwhelming amount of time needed for academic work. In some cases, if you are receiving financial aid, the amount you receive can be increased, especially if you can prove dire need. If, for example, your aid package included a family contribution that is no longer available, your financial aid counselor may be open to revising your aid eligibility. Still another option is to supplement your income with a part time or flex-time job. Be sure to check with your financial aid counselor, however. Additional earnings may affect your present or future aid package.

The alternative to increasing your income is to reduce your expenses. Certain expenses are fixed (tuition, fees, rent); others are flexible (food, entertainment, nonessential purchases). If your budget doesn't balance, your reductions must take place among the flexible budget components.

Remember, a budget is only useful it if conforms to your lifestyle. It must realistically reflect your personal needs and priorities. If, for example, you've outlined a budget that depends heavily on doing all your own cooking but your academic schedule has no leeway for spending that amount of time in the kitchen, then you're only adding additional stress to your life by expecting something of yourself you can't possibly hope to deliver. On the other hand, food is a good area in which to economize if your budget needs trimming. A $6 burger in a restaurant can be made at home for one-quarter that amount.

# COMMON SENSE BUDGET PLANNING

Six categories you should give attention to when planning your budget are housing, food, transportation, utilities and telephone, credit cards, and books. With a little creativity, you can often save considerable amounts of money in these categories.

After tuition, housing is usually the second highest component of total education cost. There are several ways you might be able to reduce your housing cost. First, you might decide to live at home or with a relative and reap the benefits of free housing. Beyond the family, you might check the employment referral service at your school. Often you can find jobs that will exchange work for free board (or reduced rent). The best example of this is child care. You might be able to exchange three or four nights of baby-sitting for free rent. One Georgetown student, for example, found a listing of Bed and Breakfasts in Washington, D.C. He then exchanged work (taking reservations) in the evenings in exchange for free board. Colleges and universities also often offer jobs that have housing benefits. For example, many schools offer residence assistant, residence director, and residence hall monitor positions. These positions often provide free housing and a modest salary in exchange for monitoring a dormitory of undergraduate students. If you go the traditional route and have to pay rent, look for a roommate to cut your costs. When you are searching for housing, look for apartments with cheaper rent. Often, if you are willing to live a little further away from campus, you can benefit from lower rates.

The key to savings when it comes to food is cooking. Ordering in and eating out should be reserved for special occasions because of their high cost compared to cooking for yourself. If you are at school for long periods of time during the day, bring your lunch. When shopping for food, shop at grocery stores and wholesale stores. Shopping at specialty shops and convenience stores is not cost effective. It is a good idea to go to the grocery store on a regular basis, perhaps once a week. Also, remember that the cheapest foods are usually the most nutritious. Rice, beans, pasta, potatoes, chicken, fresh fruits, and vegetables are just a few of these cheap nutritious foods. Nonperishable items can be bought in bulk at the beginning of the semester, or maybe once a month, to save additional money. Remember that good nutrition should be an integral part of your overall education.

Cut transportation costs by not owning a car. A car is a big expense that can cut into savings or force you to work when you should be studying. Insurance, gas, and repairs are three reasons not to own a car. Instead of taking the bus, you might consider using a bicycle. You might even consider walking to school. Riding a bike or walking to school can often replace your daily workout, saving time later in the day.

Utility and telephone costs can also be easily kept to a minimum by following some basic common sense rules. Turn the lights and air conditioner or heater off when you leave the house. Keep the heat at 68 degrees instead of 72 degrees in the winter and wear a sweater. Try to make long distance phone calls at hours when the rates are lower. You can comparison shop among telephone companies for the best long-distance rates.

Credit cards are problematic for many graduate students. The best advice regarding using a credit card is not to use one, or if you do use your credit card often, use it like a checking account. Only spend money that you have. If possible, save credit cards for emergencies and to pay the full balance every month to avoid high interest payments. Compare credit card companies for the lowest interest rate and annual fee available. Another modern card that can dip into your savings is your ATM card. You may have to pay $.50 to $1.00 just to use your ATM card. Therefore, try to use your ATM card at locations that offer free transactions.

Books and supplies are another category in which you can save significantly. Try to get your professors to put the books you will be using on reserve in the library. You can also see if the books are available at the library or through an intra-library loan system. If you are going to buy the books, try to buy used books from a student who has previously taken the class. Schools often have book co-ops or have used books at the bookstore. At the end of the semester, sell the books you will not need again.

The above areas are just some ways to stretch your budget. The key to saving money and living within your means is to be creative and not to be afraid to try new things.

# MANAGING YOUR DEBT

Principle number three in your financial planning is managing any debts you may have. Debt is manageable or unmanageable only when considered in terms of the following five things:

1. your future income
2. the amount of time it takes to repay the loan
3. the interest rate you're being charged
4. your personal lifestyle after graduation
5. unexpected circumstances which alter either your income or the ability to repay what you borrowed

"For the first year after graduation, I would certainly have referred to my debt burden as manageable," says Peter Masiello, a lawyer with one of the largest firms in San Francisco. "Then my wife and I got divorced and, suddenly, I was faced with handling my significant law school debts from just *my* salary, not our combined income. Now, two years later, I'm back on top of the situation. But for a while, I was juggling every penny I could get my hands on."

In estimating what is and what is not a manageable level of educational debt, the conservative guideline is to borrow an amount that requires no more than 5 to 8 percent of your first-year gross starting salary after graduation. Less conservative guidelines put that figure at closer to 15 percent.

Before you assume any level of debt, however, you should know as much as you can about what you are borrowing, what will be expected of you, and alternatives to borrowing. This requires thoroughly understanding your school's financial aid policy. You should know the following:

- the school's criteria for who qualifies for financial aid
- maximum aid amounts awarded by the school
- how much self-help money will be expected of you
- alternative ways to handle unmet need

One essential ingredient of any program of debt management is record keeping. With the reality of having three or four loans included as part of your financial aid package, just keeping track of how much you owe and to whom becomes a challenge. See the chart on page 28 for an example of a workable loan record form.

# CREDIT CARDS

Much has been written warning students about the hazards of credit cards. My colleague, Ruth-Lammeot-Reeves, Assistant Dean for Financial Aid at Georgetown Law Center says it best. The following seven pages contain Ruth's advice about credit card use. I am certain you will find it informative.

An increasing number of students have made use of credit cards while in graduate school. Many students develop a credit card habit during their undergraduate years and accelerate their spending while in school. Many of these students do not know how to manage their credit card debts; they do not realize the negative impact mismanaged credit has on future financial choices. Following a few simple guidelines will help you avoid the pitfalls experienced by other students.

### If You Must Use Credit—A Few Guidelines

- Use credit cards only when you have the resources to cover the bill when it arrives. Running your card up to the credit limit and then struggling to pay even the monthly payment is financially dangerous.

## Loan Record

| Name of Loan | Amt. Borrowed | Int. Rate | Terms and Conditions | Min. Pmt. Month | Total Pmt. Year |
|---|---|---|---|---|---|
| 1. Federal Perkins | _____ | ___% | Grace= <br> Deferment = <br> Repayt.= ____ yrs. | _____ | _____ |
| 2. Federal Subsidized Stafford | _____ | ___% | Grace = <br> Deferment = <br> Repayt. = ___ yrs. | _____ | _____ |
| 3. Federal Unsubsidized Stafford | _____ | ___% | Grace = <br> Deferment = <br> Repayt. = ___ yrs. | _____ | _____ |
| 4. Other | _____ | ___% | Grace = <br> Deferment = <br> Repayt. = ___ yrs. | _____ | _____ |
| 5. Other | _____ | ___% | Grace = <br> Deferment = <br> Repayt.=___yrs. | _____ | _____ |

- Credit card debt should not exceed 10 percent of your gross monthly income. This means that if your job pays $400 per month, you should limit your credit card charges to $40 per month.

- Don't miss a credit card payment, no matter how small. If you do, you'll pay interest on all new purchases not just the unpaid balance. Also a lender reviewing your prior payment record will perceive you as a poor risk if you are unable to keep your bills current.

- Don't think the excuses "I moved," "I was sick," or "I was busy with exams" are acceptable reasons for missing payments. They aren't. Learn from other students' mistakes—their loan applications were rejected, and yours will be too if you miss payments.

- Don't fall into the trap and overspend by charging all your expenses in order to keep up. Students with high credit card debt often can manage only the minimum monthly payment, if that. And the interest charges are exorbitant.

## The Pitfalls of Using Credit Cards

- Credit card debts tie up future income.

- It is easy to overspend when you use "plastic."

- The interest charged costs money you can ill afford.

- Nonpayment results in a spoiled credit rating. This stays with you for a long time and can affect your eligibility for future student and consumer loans.

- Your student budget cannot be increased to cover either monthly credit card payments, prior debt, or excessive spending while in graduate school.

## Go "Cold Turkey" on Credit Card Use

- If you've been working and return to school as a full time student, obviously you no longer have the regular income you did when working. Your spending habits must immediately reflect this change. The first step in cutting your spending is to stop using your credit cards.

- Credit card withdrawal process should start several months, or even a year, before the semester begins, especially if you're carrying a balance. The first step is payment of all your outstanding credit obligations so that you have no debts hanging over your head once school gets underway.

- Limiting credit card use to emergency purchases, or cut up all your credit cards if you know you'll have difficulty limiting your spending. In any case, you should winnow the number of credit cards you have to two. If possible, you should not carry these cards with you. They should be kept in a safe place, available when needed for a specific legitimate purchase.

Following these general guidelines will help you avoid the financial difficulties other students have experienced and allow you more control over your finances.

# HOW IMPORTANT IS YOUR CREDIT HISTORY?

Too many students who have applied for a "commercial" student loan, e.g., Law Access, LawLoans, or GradShare/GradExcel loans, have had an unwelcome entry to the world of consumer credit. Their loans were denied because of their credit records. While some loan denials are correctable, others are not, especially if a credit history is accurate and payments have been missed. Frequently, students only realize when it is too late that their credit history is a very important credential. Late payment, nonpayment, and charge-off information stays on your credit report for seven years and could seriously damage your financial options.

To take advantage of all the financing alternatives for graduate school expenses, a pristine credit record is mandatory. A prior negative history will jeopardize eligibility for commercial student loans. A lender sees past actions as an indication of how a borrower will behave in the future. If a credit report shows missed payments in the past, a potential lender presumes that the borrower will do the same in the future. An applicant with a record of credit problems will be considered a "bad risk" and will be denied a loan. In addition, some states find law school graduates with poor credit histories "unfit" to sit for the bar exam!

## Worried About Your Credit History? Find Out Before You Apply

How good is your credit? Don't assume that just because you recently received an offer for a credit card in the mail that your credit history is good enough to receive a commercial student loan. You should know that certain credit card vendors may target people who are frequent late payers so they can charge late fees in addition to interest, thus increasing their profitability margin. The commercial student loan lenders are not in this group. They do not look favorably on applications from late or delinquent payers. Credit criteria for loans is determined by the individual lender. The most liberal lender will allow one 90-day late payment within the last year. Other private lenders allow no more than two 60-day late payments (and none any later). And some lenders use even more stringent guidelines.

If you are planning to apply for a commercial student loan and are uncertain about what your credit report will say, find out if there are any problems ahead of time and see if you can correct them before your lender considers your application.

You should obtain a copy of your credit history from your local credit bureau or one of three national credit bureaus several months before sending the loan application to the Financial Aid Office for processing.

Although neutral or positive information about your repayment history may vary among credit bureaus, negative items seem to be consistently reported to all three national agencies. These agencies are the following: CBI (also known as CBI/Equifax), Trans Union Corp., and TRW. You may obtain information on the request process by calling CBI/Equifax at 800-685-1111, Trans Union at 216-779-7200, or TRW at 800-392-1122. Contact them for information on fees (usually $5-$15, but some are free of charge) and to find out if you need to submit any other identification when writing your request letter. (If you wish to be extremely thorough, obtain copies from all three agencies.)

Once you obtain the credit report, review it for accuracy. If you have blemishes on your record, do what you can to rectify them. No lender will consider you for a loan if you have an outstanding judgment, a lien, or an open charge-off (an account that was closed for nonpayment). This information stays in your file for seven years and stays with you even if you move from state to state. If you pay off an outstanding obligation, it usually takes at least one year of good credit history to offset the blemish. You will not be able to pay off a debt and then immediately be approved for a new loan. The prospective creditor wants proof that whatever occurred in the past will not be repeated. A year of good payments is the minimum length of time.

## Suggestions for Student Loan Denials Based on Credit

If you are denied a commercial student loan, there are several steps you should follow to try to qualify. Take action immediately when you learn you have been denied. Do not wait until your rent is overdue and your phone has been shut off. Successful appeals take time and require a lot of legwork.

1. Find out what credit bureau provided the report the lender used to deny you credit. Contact the lender to obtain this information. Federal law requires a lender to notify a loan applicant in writing when credit is denied. That letter should specify the credit bureau where your credit record was obtained. (Each lender uses the credit bureau of its choice.) If you learn of your denial by phone you should ask for the name and address of the credit bureau that was used. No lender will

tell you the specifics about what is in your credit record. You must obtain a copy of the report directly from the credit bureau.

2. Write a letter to the credit bureau requesting a copy of your report immediately. If you submit your written request within thirty days of being denied a loan, the report will be free. To ensure receiving a free report it is a good idea to enclose a copy of the denial letter from the lender. You should begin the credit appeal and review process as soon as possible. Contact the credit bureau concerning the fees and to learn if there are any other procedures you should follow; policies differ depending on the agency and the region of the country. In some instances, a credit bureau will ask you to provide a copy of your driver's license along with your request.

3. Review your credit report for factual errors. Is someone else's negative information listed on your report? (Sometimes people with similar names encounter this problem.) Or are some of the credit entries inaccurate? If there are inaccuracies, you have the right to dispute them, and the bureau must recheck the item. If you know the item is wrong, you should go to the source credit card company, or bank and ask them to correct the error. If the item is reverified, you can have the dispute included in your file by writing a letter to the credit bureau. Unfortunately, you may find yourself bouncing between the bureau and the company or store trying to get the matter corrected. Once the matter is corrected, be sure to have the company send you a copy of the letter. Ask that the correction be sent to all three agencies. The next time you apply for credit you may have to repeat the entire procedure if you didn't obtain a copy of the letter and the correction went to a different credit agency.

4. Armed with the information obtained from your credit report, write an appeal letter to your lender. Note that several lenders have policies stating that your application will not be considered unless you can document factual errors that have been corrected on your credit file. Make an appointment with a financial aid counselor to review your credit report and the approach you plan to take in your appeal. Do this as soon as you can after learning you have been denied the loan and obtained your record from the credit bureau. Financial aid counselors have no power to expunge the credit records of their students and neither does anyone else. Counselors work with students to give them the best information they have on

successful approaches and alternative solutions. The best way to deal with this problem is to avoid it altogether. Treat your credit history as carefully as you do your grade point average.

If you would like more information on sound credit card practices, how to avoid being taken advantage of by credit card companies, and what your rights are under the Fair Credit Act, call the Bankcard Holders of America 703-389-5445, a nonprofit consumer advocacy group, for more information.

## Clean Your Credit File?

Some of the come-on ads say, "start over—brand new credit file" or "no matter how bad your credit record, we can help you." Students who damage their credit files mistakenly believe that simply by going to a credit file "doctor" or other service and paying a fee, their credit reports will be swept clean of all prior negative information.

There is *no legal way* for information such as unpaid bills, late payments, canceled debt, write-offs for bad debt, and the like to be miraculously removed from a person's credit report. Information remains on a credit file for seven years. The passage of time is the only cure, and this assumes the offending bills have been paid and no additional negative credit actions have occurred.

A company considering lending an applicant money for a car loan or granting a line of credit sets its own guidelines for how far back it will look into an applicant's credit activity to determine a good risk. With student loans, the shortest time frame is twelve months after all credit problems have been corrected, before additional credit will be approved. This is for the most liberal lender.

A "credit doctor" may be a scam, where an organization takes your money and does nothing, or one that provides a "secured" card. In the instance of the scam, you are required to pay a large fee and are promised a clean record. You receive nothing for your payment except perhaps a list of organizations that will provide loans at interest rates in excess of 20 percent. These "doctors" have no legal way of deleting negative information from any of the three national credit agencies or their affiliates, and simply prey upon people who are already in a financial bind.

In the second instance, you will be asked, for example, to deposit $500 or more into a bank account. You are then able to make credit purchases up to the amount in the bank account. Although this arrangement allows you to have a credit card, it does not eliminate information about prior credit problems from your credit record. Nor does it mean you will be able to obtain other forms of credit such as commercial student loans.

The only proven method of avoiding credit card scams such as these is to never need to go to the "doctor" in the first place. If you can't afford to pay for it, don't buy it hoping that somehow you'll find the money when the credit card bill arrives.

# SUMMER PAYMENTS ARE MONITORED

If you are going to be away during the summer, you cannot simply ignore your credit card and other bills and plan to "catch them up" when you return. Make arrangements for the bills to be paid. Each time you apply for a commercial student loan, the lender reviews your credit file. Because you were approved for a commercial loan last year doesn't mean your application will be automatically approved in the future. You must pay your bills responsibly at all times, not just during the academic year.

If you are going on a summer trip overseas, leave postdated checks for the estimated payment amount and arrange for a friend or relative to handle your bills and mail while you're gone. If you can't afford to make the payments to keep your bills current, you can't afford the trip!

If you are relocating in the U.S. during the summer, contact your credit companies and have your billing address changed. Students who have left mail forwarding requests at the U.S. Postal Office have had mixed results. If you rely on your summer subleaser to forward your mail, you will inevitably have problems. An absentminded subleaser can jeopardize your credit rating. If you know that you have not received a monthly billing statement from one of your credit companies, contact them. Your bill is going somewhere; by the time you receive it, you could have already been assessed late fees and penalties, and the missed payments will appear as negative information on your credit report.

Source: *Georgetown University Law Center Financial Aid Guidebook* 1995-96.

# LOAN REPAYMENT

The chart provided on pages 37 and 38 are condensed versions of what you might find if you thumbed through professional volumes on debt repayment. The information serves two purposes: it allows you to determine quickly and without knowing the ins and outs of debt repayment what you will be expected to pay monthly and yearly, and it provides a perspective on your debt compared to the projections for what you will be earning after graduation. Loan payments for a given amount are determined by the interest rate at which you received the loan and the number of years it will take for you to pay it back.

Annual interest rates from 3 percent to 9 percent are listed across the top of each column of figures. Durations of loan repayment are listed down the left side and extend from one year to ten years. To find the monthly or annual payment required on a $1,000 loan at 7 percent interest for ten years, find the 7 percent column, run down to the row of figures labeled ten years at the left of the page. From there, you'll see that $11.61 represents the monthly payment and $139.32 represents the annual payment. It's important to remember, however, that most loan programs have established $50 as the minimum monthly payment. If your interest rate falls between the rates listed, take the next higher and the next lower and figure out an amount in between. If the original $1000 was given to you at 7.5 percent interest, for example, your monthly payment would be halfway between $11.61 and $12.13, or $11.87. Your annual payment would be halfway between $139.32 and $145.56, or $142.44.

Because many students have no clear understanding of what percent of their future salary will be needed for loan repayments, the two tables on pages 37 and 38 illustrate how much of your future earnings will be needed to make payments on a $10,000 loan over either ten or twenty years. Seven starting salaries are listed down the left side of the page. In the next column, each starting salary is assigned four possible rates of annual increase.

Across the top are five possible loan interest rates, one for each column of figures. The figures that correspond represent the amount of your loan as a percentage of your salary over time for a specific interest rate. Let's say, for example, that you borrowed $10,000 for ten years at 7 percent interest. Let's also say that your starting salary is $30,000, and that for the next ten years you get annual salary increases of 4 percent. Extrapolating from the first chart, after ten years you would assume a debt burden of 3.87 percent of your salary. If you borrowed $10,000 for twenty years with the same starting salary and the same rate of annual salary increase, your debt burden would fall to 2.08 percent of your salary.

If you borrow any amount other than $10,000, divide that amount by 10,000, and multiply the appropriate figure from the table by the result. If, for example, you borrow $15,000 at 7 percent for ten years and your starting salary is $20,000, with annual increases of 6 percent: 15,000 divided by 10,000 = 1.5; 1.5 times 5.29 (the figure extrapolated from the 10-year repayment table) = 7.84, which represents the percentage of your salary required to repay the loan. Interest rates, starting salary rates, and salary increase rates that do not appear in the tables can be figured out by interpolating between the available figures.

Remember, debt is manageable only in relation to how much you'll be earning. If there's a question in your mind as to typical earnings in the field you're considering, check with the college placement office or the Chamber of Commerce in the city where you plan to work. Better still, talk to other graduates in that field. Find out the range of salaries, the possibilities for salary increases, and the availability of jobs in the field. The absolute worst-case scenario would be to graduate with debt and find there are no jobs available for you.

## Ten (10) Year Repayment

**Percent of Cumulative Salary Required to Repay $10,000 Loan
in Ten Years by Constant Monthly Repayment**

| Starting Salary | Annual Salary Increase | 3% | 5% | 7% | 8% | 9% |
|---|---|---|---|---|---|---|
| $20,000 | 2% | 5.29 | 5.81 | 6.36 | 6.65 | 6.94 |
| | 4% | 4.83 | 5.30 | 5.80 | 6.06 | 6.33 |
| | 6% | 4.40 | 4.83 | 5.29 | 5.52 | 5.77 |
| | 10% | 3.64 | 3.99 | 4.37 | 4.57 | 4.77 |
| $25,000 | 2% | 4.23 | 4.65 | 5.09 | 5.32 | 5.55 |
| | 4% | 3.86 | 4.24 | 4.64 | 4.85 | 5.06 |
| | 6% | 3.52 | 3.86 | 4.23 | 4.42 | 4.61 |
| | 10% | 2.91 | 3.19 | 3.50 | 3.65 | 3.82 |
| $30,000 | 2% | 3.53 | 3.87 | 4.24 | 4.43 | 4.63 |
| | 4% | 3.22 | 3.53 | 3.87 | 4.04 | 4.22 |
| | 6% | 2.93 | 3.22 | 3.52 | 3.68 | 3.84 |
| | 10% | 2.42 | 2.66 | 2.91 | 3.05 | 3.18 |
| $35,000 | 2% | 3.02 | 3.32 | 3.64 | 3.80 | 3.97 |
| | 4% | 2.76 | 3.03 | 3.32 | 3.46 | 3.62 |
| | 6% | 2.51 | 2.76 | 3.05 | 3.16 | 3.30 |
| | 10% | 2.08 | 2.28 | 2.50 | 2.61 | 2.73 |
| $40,000 | 2% | 2.65 | 2.91 | 3.18 | 3.32 | 3.47 |
| | 4% | 2.41 | 2.65 | 2.90 | 3.03 | 3.17 |
| | 6% | 2.20 | 2.41 | 2.64 | 2.76 | 2.88 |
| | 10% | 1.82 | 2.00 | 2.19 | 2.28 | 2.38 |
| $75,000 | 2% | 1.41 | 1.55 | 1.70 | 1.77 | 1.85 |
| | 4% | 1.29 | 1.41 | 1.55 | 1.62 | 1.69 |
| | 6% | 1.17 | 1.29 | 1.41 | 1.47 | 1.54 |
| | 10% | 0.97 | 1.06 | 1.17 | 1.22 | 1.27 |
| $100,000 | 2% | 1.06 | 1.16 | 1.27 | 1.33 | 1.39 |
| | 4% | 0.97 | 1.06 | 1.16 | 1.21 | 1.27 |
| | 6% | 0.88 | 0.97 | 1.06 | 1.10 | 1.15 |
| | 10% | 0.73 | 0.80 | 0.87 | 0.91 | 0.95 |

# Twenty (20) Year Repayment

**Percent of Cumulative Salary Required to Repay $10,000 Loan
in Twenty Years by Constant Monthly Repayments**

| Starting Salary | Annual Salary Increase | 3% | 5% | 7% | 8% | 9% |
|---|---|---|---|---|---|---|
| $20,000 | 2% | 2.74 | 3.26 | 3.83 | 4.13 | 4.44 |
| | 4% | 2.23 | 2.66 | 3.12 | 3.37 | 3.63 |
| | 6% | 1.81 | 2.15 | 2.53 | 2.73 | 2.94 |
| | 10% | 1.16 | 1.38 | 1.62 | 1.75 | 1.89 |
| $25,000 | 2% | 2.19 | 2.61 | 3.06 | 3.30 | 3.55 |
| | 4% | 1.79 | 2.13 | 2.50 | 2.70 | 2.90 |
| | 6% | 1.45 | 1.72 | 2.02 | 2.18 | 2.35 |
| | 10% | 0.93 | 1.11 | 1.30 | 1.40 | 1.51 |
| $30,000 | 2% | 1.83 | 2.17 | 2.55 | 2.75 | 2.96 |
| | 4% | 1.49 | 1.77 | 2.08 | 2.25 | 2.42 |
| | 6% | 1.21 | 1.44 | 1.69 | 1.82 | 1.96 |
| | 10% | 0.77 | 0.92 | 1.08 | 1.17 | 1.26 |
| $35,000 | 2% | 1.57 | 1.86 | 2.19 | 2.36 | 2.54 |
| | 4% | 1.28 | 1.52 | 1.79 | 1.93 | 2.07 |
| | 6% | 1.03 | 1.23 | 1.45 | 1.56 | 1.68 |
| | 10% | 0.66 | 0.79 | 0.93 | 1.00 | 1.08 |
| $40,000 | 2% | 1.37 | 1.63 | 1.91 | 2.07 | 2.22 |
| | 4% | 1.12 | 1.33 | 1.56 | 1.69 | 1.81 |
| | 6% | 0.90 | 1.08 | 1.26 | 1.36 | 1.47 |
| | 10% | 0.58 | 0.69 | 0.81 | 0.88 | 0.94 |
| $75,000 | 2% | 0.73 | 0.87 | 1.02 | 1.10 | 1.18 |
| | 4% | 0.60 | 0.71 | 0.83 | 0.90 | 0.97 |
| | 6% | 0.48 | 0.57 | 0.67 | 0.73 | 0.78 |
| | 10% | 0.31 | 0.37 | 0.43 | 0.47 | 0.50 |
| $100,000 | 2% | 0.55 | 0.65 | 0.77 | 0.83 | 0.89 |
| | 4% | 0.45 | 0.53 | 0.62 | 0.67 | 0.73 |
| | 6% | 0.36 | 0.43 | 0.51 | 0.55 | 0.59 |
| | 10% | 0.23 | 0.28 | 0.32 | 0.35 | 0.38 |

**Student Loan Counselor Software**

The *Student Loan Counselor* is a debt management software package developed by the Educational Testing Service (ETS) for the Graduate and Professional School Financial Aid Council and sold to schools and libraries around the country. The program asks the user a series of questions relating to previous indebtedness, career plans, etc., showing the relationship between current borrowing and future income. It stresses the need for careful planning. Check with your school to see if it has a copy you can use. It is also available in some libraries.

Several other student loan software packages are now available. Both the Access Group and United Student Aid Group recently have released software packages to help you manage your debt. And the Internet offers debt management counseling as well.

## Loan Consolidation

Loan consolidation is a loan program designed to simplify a borrower's payment of educational loans. Through consolidation, you can combine eligible educational loans into one single loan that requires only one monthly payment often less than the total amount you'd have to pay on multiple loans. This consolidated loan also permits you to extend the repayment period, which can reduce the monthly payments (although, keep in mind that it also increases the total amount of interest you pay). Loans eligible for consolidation include:

- Subsidized Federal Stafford Loans (formerly called GSL),
- Unsubsidized Federal Stafford Loans,
- Federal Supplemental Loans for Students (SLS),
- Federal PLUS Loans that you borrowed for your dependent children,
- Federally Insured Student Loans (FISL),
- Federal Perkins Loans (formerly called NDSL),
- Health Professions Student Loans (HPSL),
- Health Education Assistance Loans (HEAL), and
- Nursing Student Loans (administered by U.S. Department of Health and Human Services).

Currently, there is no federal minimum balance requirement for a consolidation loan. All loans to be consolidated must either be in a grace period or in repayment status. If you have a delinquent or defaulted loan, you still may be eligible for consolidation but only if you reenter repayment through loan consolidation. The interest rate you pay on a consolidation loan is the weighted average interest rate of all loans being consolidated, rounded upward to the nearest whole percent. The maximum number of years you have to repay your consolidation loan is based on the amount you owe. The following table shows the maximum repayment term for a consolidation loan.

## Maximum Repayment Terms for Consolidation Loans

| Balance | Maximum Number of Years |
|---|---|
| less than $7,500 | 10 |
| $7,500–$9,999 | 12 |
| $10,000–$19,999 | 15 |
| $20,000–$39,999 | 20 |
| $40,000–$59,000 | 25 |
| $60,000 and greater | 30 |

There are benefits of loan consolidation. First, you pay a single monthly payment for the consolidated loan that is often less than the total you pay on multiple loans. Second, you can reduce your monthly payment, either by increasing the number of years to repay the loan, using a graduated repayment schedule, or by lowering the interest rate on a PLUS or SLS loan. Third, the consolidation loan may be eligible for subsidized deferments under certain conditions.

If you did not include any eligible outstanding loans at the time you consolidated, for up to 180 days after you consolidate you may add them to your consolidation loan. Married couples may jointly consolidate their eligible loans, but both borrowers are jointly and severally liable for repayment of the loan.

While consolidation can be very helpful, there are also costs associated with it. And, sometimes, the consolidation interest rate is higher than the interest rate you are paying. Also, keep in mind that if the repayment term is extended, you will pay more total interest. And, you will lose several deferment options available on subsidized Stafford, unsubsidized Stafford, SLS, PLUS, Perkins, and HPSL loans.

## Federal Direct Consolidation Loan Program

This program establishes an Individual Education Account (IEA) that allows you to combine multiple federal education loans (or even one loan) into a new single account to make repayment easier. This is also called refinancing.

There are several benefits of an Individual Education Account. Like the consolidation loan, you (and your spouse, if you consolidate jointly) will have only one payment to make each month for all loans you consolidate.

Second, the interest rate on the consolidation loan may be lower than the interest rate you are paying on your loan, which reduces the amount you repay monthly.

Third, you can choose from among several options to repay your loan including some that may allow you up to thirty years to repay. Other repayment plans based on your income allow you up to twenty-five years to repay. If your financial situation changes, you may change your repayment option.

The variable interest rate will never exceed 8.25 percent if you are a student borrower, or 9 percent if you are a parent (PLUS Loan) borrower.

The following federal education loans may be included in an IEA:

- Federal Direct and FFEL Stafford Loans (subsidized and unsubsidized),
- Federal Direct and FFEL PLUS Loans,
- Federal Direct and FFEL Consolidation Loans,
- Guaranteed Student Loans (GSL),
- Federal Insured Student Loans (FISL),
- Federal Supplemental Loans for Students (SLS),
- Auxiliary Loans to Assist Students (ALAS),
- Federal Perkins Loans, and
- National Direct/National Defense Student Loans (NDSL)

Health and Human Services Loans may also be included in an IEA. These loans are:

- Nursing Student Loans,
- Primary Care Loans, and
- Health Education Assistance Loans (HEAL)

There are four ways to repay your IEA.

1. Standard Repayment Option. Under this option, you'll be required to pay a fixed amount (at least $50) each month for up to ten years. Your actual payment amount and repayment period will depend on your loan amount.
2. Extended Repayment Option. Under this option, you'll be allowed to extend your repayment over a period of twelve to thirty years, depending on your loan amount. Your fixed monthly payment (at least $50) may be lower than it would be under the Standard Repayment Option, but you'll repay a higher total amount of interest because the repayment period is longer.
3. Graduated Repayment Option. Under this option, your payments will be lower at first and then increase every two years over a period of time ranging from twelve to thirty years. The actual length of your repayment depends on your loan amount. However, you'll repay a higher total amount of interest than under the Standard Repayment Option because the repayment period is longer.
4. Income Contingent Repayment Option. Under this option, your monthly payment is based on your annual income, family size, and loan amount. As your income rises or falls, so do your payments. You can take up to twenty-five years to repay your IEA under the income contingent repayment option. After twenty-five years, any remaining balance on your IEA will be forgiven, although you will have to pay tax on any amount forgiven. Note that the longer you take to repay your IEA, the more interest you will have to pay.

# REDUCING YOUR PAYMENT— ALTERNATIVES

If you find you must borrow more money than is reasonably manageable to make it through graduate school, you should think about alternatives.

Loan consolidation is an alternative for federal student loans. Alternative payment plans and prepayment are possibilities for federal and private student loans.

*Alternative Payment Plans:* Many lenders offer alternative payment plans when loans are consolidated. You can, for example, pay only the interest for a period of time, an arrangement that substantially lowers the monthly payment. In two years, when your salary has increased to a level where you can afford to make full payments, the plan reverts to its original arrangement whereby you pay interest and principal on a monthly basis. The advantage of this arrangement is that it offers you flexibility when you need it most—early in your career when your salary is lowest. The disadvantage is that you ultimately pay a greater amount of interest. A similar plan offered by some lenders is a graduated payment based on salary. As in the above plan, you initially pay only the interest plus a small amount toward the principal. Gradually, as your salary rises, the monthly payments increase until the full amount is repaid.

*Prepayment:* Most loan programs allow you to pay off the balance at any point without penalty. If, for example, you're given a salary bonus, come into an inheritance, or find that you borrowed more than you needed and have money left over, it's in your best interest to make accelerated payments on your loans. By doing this, your principal is reduced, thereby reducing the overall amount of monthly payment.

# REDUCING YOUR DEBT

The best way to keep your debts manageable is to borrow less. Here are a few ways to keep your debt burden down.

*Limit Student Borrowing:* Many students decide to take out all the loans for which they are eligible. In some cases they overestimate the amount they need. In other cases, they're convinced it will be in their best interest to borrow the money and reinvest it in something paying greater interest. Besides being against the terms of the loan (which say the money can only be used for school-related purposes), this manner of thinking is most often wrong. Loan rates hover in the 7 to 10 percent range. Investments paying more than that amount are usually risky and can jeopardize your long-term financial well-being.

*Family Financing:* Although most graduate students are considered to be independent with respect to qualifying for federal financial aid, many families are still willing and able to assist in paying for education. This is especially true if families understand that their money reduces student debt. While parents or family members may be unable or unwilling to provide grant assistance, they may be willing and able to provide a loan, often with more attractive terms than federal and private loans. Such loans, however, may have tax consequences. A tax adviser should be consulted before obtaining a loan from someone in your family.

*Early Graduation/Summer School:* It is possible to reduce total indebtedness by completing your education more quickly than originally intended. You may take more courses per semester. Or you may attend classes in the summer in addition to your semester schedule, although this option would reduce the time you are able to work during the summer.

*Attending Part Time:* You may, conversely, decide to enroll for less than a full semester, thereby leaving time for yourself to work. Remember though, to qualify for most student aid you must be enrolled at least half time, which is usually six credits per term. Students attending less than half time must begin paying off their loans immediately; or, in the case of Federal Stafford and Federal Perkins Loans, you begin the grace period and then start repaying the loan when the grace period has expired.

# WHO QUALIFIES FOR AID AND HOW IS ELIGIBILITY DETERMINED?

ina Chang remembers her initial misapprehensions about graduate school financial aid: "When I first realized I'd need much more money than what I had to even remotely contemplate law school, I thought, 'forget about it—most graduate school aid is based on having been a straight A student.' Not that I didn't have my share of A's; but I also had a generous sprinkling of B's. A friend finally convinced me to go talk to a financial aid counselor, and it was then I learned I could get money simply because I needed it."

The kind of misapprehensions Tina originally had are common but, fortunately, not always valid. Graduate school financial aid, especially at a professional school such as law, medicine, or business, is based largely on the determination of what a student needs to attend a particular institution; this is what we'll be calling *need-based aid.*

Graduate programs for master's degree candidates may offer some need-based aid, but often they do not have adequate support to meet the full financial need of their students, and they expect their students to find their own ways of filling the gap in their aid packages.

For some fields of study, particularly in Ph.D. programs in arts and sciences at major research universities like Harvard, where I spent fourteen years administering financial aid programs, students could get *merit-based aid* in the form of grants to cover all of their tuition and living expenses. However, this level of funding, often committed for the duration of the degree program, sometimes as long as six years, is probably the exception, not the rule, at most universities.

There are also some fellowship programs available for certain groups of students. This so-called *targeted aid* is awarded to attract certain populations of students to study in an area where perhaps they have been underrepresented in the past. For example, the U.S. Department of Education has grants for minority students who plan to pursue a Ph.D.

So when you're thinking about going to graduate school, keep in mind that graduate financial aid may be awarded either on the basis of need, according to your academic merit, or because you are a member of a group that has traditionally been underrepresented in a particular field.

## Graduate vs. Undergraduate Aid

Graduate financial aid is different from a great deal of the undergraduate aid that is available in that much of it is merit-based; that is, grants are given to students who the academic department is interested in having attend its program. Doctoral programs in science have much more grant money to offer than those in, say, musicology, while professional degree students (medicine, law, business) should be prepared to borrow significant amounts.

This merit-based support is often in the form of a fellowship that may or may not have a service-related component (such as a teaching assistantship or a research assistantship). Most of these awards are given by the academic department, and many of them are for Ph.D. students. Consult your academic department or the graduate school office of the school you're interested in to see if it awards merit-based aid, and, if so, what process it uses to award these funds.

## Graduate Aid vs. Undergraduate Aid

*On the positive side:*

1. Graduate schools and federal and state governments understand the difficulty of financing graduate education. As a result, there are several federal, state, and local graduate school programs that offer support to graduate students.
2. The attractiveness of state university graduate programs has grown enormously because their tuition and fees can be less than half that of private programs.
3. Finally, military programs have expanded their financial aid to graduate students who have been with or pledge to be with the service.

*Some of the drawbacks:*

1. Graduate education can be more expensive than undergraduate school, primarily because it's more labor-intensive than undergraduate education. Generally there are no large lecture courses and graduate students often work closely with faculty members, sometimes even one-to-one.

2. Most graduate schools lack the extensively endowed scholarship programs of undergraduate institutions and, therefore, cannot always make a commitment to provide aid to all who qualify for admission. As a result, aid is limited and very competitive. Only the top research institutions have the funds to finance the students they want in their graduate programs.

3. Graduate students frequently arrive with an undergraduate debt burden, making them less willing or less able to assume additional debt.

4. Part-time work is less feasible for graduate students because of the heavy academic burden imposed by graduate programs.

Source: adapted from Howard Greene and Robert Minton, *Behind the Ivy Wall*, Little, Brown, 1989.

## Targeted Aid

There are some special programs earmarked for certain groups of students. For example, the National Science Foundation offers fellowships for doctoral students studying in the natural, physical, biological, and social sciences. Ford Foundation Fellowships are available for minority students and women underrepresented in certain fields of study. There are also loans available for those studying for specific degrees, the J.D., and the M.B.A. If you fit one of these categories, refer to Chapter 6, which contains more information about special aid programs for specific student populations. Also see the appendix for directories, data-bases, and other sources of information.

# NEED-BASED AID

The main purpose of need-based aid is to lessen the cost barriers that may prevent you from pursuing your educational goals; as such it is supplemental to—but not a replacement for—what you and, in some instances, your family are expected to contribute to the cost of your education.

Most federal, state, and a great deal of institutional aid are awarded on the basis of need. Simply put, need-based aid eligibility is the difference between your cost of attendance and your financial resources. Resources may include such things as savings from summer earnings, earnings during the school year, spouse's earnings, and your savings. Financial aid eligibility is calculated by subtracting your resources from the total standard student budget at the school. You can refer to Chapter 1 for an explanation of student budgets.

The underlying philosophy of need-based graduate financial aid is that every student should have the opportunity to attain a graduate degree, regardless of his or her ability to pay for it. Supporting this concept are three principles: *access, persistence,* and *fairness*.

1. *Access.* You should have *access* to the program that best suits your academic needs. Financial considerations should not be the guiding force. Ideally, all programs should have an adequate base of funding. In reality this is not always the case.
2. *Persistence.* Once you have begun graduate school, your ability to pay should not prevent you from completing your education. If assistance has been provided to allow access, you should have reasonable assurance that aid will *persist* for the duration of your graduate program. This also is not always the case and certainly the amount and types of aid you receive can change year to year.
3. *Fairness.* Finally, you or your family's ability to pay (which figures greatly in the amount of aid you receive) should be determined *fairly*, using a standardized formula based on recent income and asset evaluation.

## Who's Income Counts Toward Financial Aid?

"I haven't lived at home for five years, yet my parents claim me on their income tax. Will the financial aid committee consider me dependent or independent?

"I live at home in order to care for my elderly mother. She pays the mortgage, and I pay the rest—the food, the insurance, the maintenance, and the repairs. Can I characterize myself as independent?

"My parents are both dead, but my sole source of support is a trust fund they set up while they were still living. Should I claim myself dependent or independent?"

What is independence? Or, more appropriately, "Am I considered independent or dependent?" This is one of the first questions you'll have to answer when you begin to complete a financial aid application. Your answer determines whether or not it's necessary to have your parents complete a portion of the form. At issue is whether you are responsible for providing your own subsistence and expenses, or whether this responsibility is to be shared by your parents *and* you. For federal aid purposes, graduate students are automatically independent.

However, graduate students are automatically independent only for federal aid. Some schools, especially medical schools, do require parental information and expect a contribution from parents who are able to provide it. Moreover, most schools expect the spouse of a graduate student to provide at least a contribution toward living expenses. You might ask, "Why is parental information required even though I am 'legally' independent?" The answer is, the greater the parents' resources, the better able you will be to deal with financial emergencies and the responsibilities of educational debt. Essentially, there are more options open to students whose parents have greater financial strength, even when direct parental subsidy is not forthcoming. For example, graduate students from wealthier families often are able to arrange a loan from their parents, rather than through banks. And these family loans often have significantly more favorable terms (such as lower interest rates or deferred payments).

Graduate schools awarding their own need-based institutional aid often want to know that the grants they provide are going to those students with no other options available to fund their graduate education. This is a very controversial topic, hotly debated on campus, and schools differ in how they award institutional aid. Consult the Financial Aid Office of your intended school to determine its policy regarding the requirement of parental data.

## How Need Is Determined

The determination of what you are expected to contribute from your resources is based on a formula provided by the U.S. Congress. This formula, called Federal Methodology, determines the amount of money you should have available for educational purposes. *Need analysis* is the process of estimating the amount of assistance you will need to supplement the resources you theoretically have available to pay for your schooling. It has two basic components: first, what it will reasonably cost you to attend a given school for a given period of time (commonly referred to as Cost of Attendance and explained in detail in Chapter 1), and second, an estimation of your ability and your family's (if applicable) to contribute to your educational costs.

## Federal Methodology (FM)

Need analysis for student federal financial aid is based on a formula called the Federal Methodology (FM). FM uses taxable and nontaxable base-year income and your assets to calculate your expected Family Contribution (FC; see below). Base year means the calendar year before that of enrollment. Thus a financial aid application for the 1996-97 academic year is based on 1995 income.

## Expected Family Contribution (EFC)

After arriving at the correct cost of attendance for you, to calculate your financial need the financial aid counselor must determine your Expected Family Contribution—the amount that you and, if applicable, your spouse can be expected to contribute to our overall educational cost. The amount you are expected to contribute should, theoretically, be the same whatever school you attend. Once your family contribution is calculated, it is subtracted from the cost of attendance, and the remaining amount is your financial need.

The resources used to calculate your family contribution include such things as savings from summer earnings, earnings during the school year, spouse's earnings, and a percentage of your total assets.

The specific components used to calculate the family contribution are: student income, including annual income as well as any dividends, interest, benefits, or untaxed income; minus student allowances such as federal, state, and social security taxes. Then, living and maintenance allowances are subtracted from income to leave an amount available for you to spend on your education. In addition, students are expected to contribute 35 percent of their assets to meet their educational expenses. Assets include savings, stocks, bonds, and real estate. If you own your home, the equity (the value minus whatever you owe on it) is *not* counted as an asset for federal aid. However, many schools *will* count home equity when awarding their own institutional aid.

## Parental Contribution Calculation

If the school you are attending requires you to submit parents' income and asset information, your parental contribution calculation will be made using some or all of the following data:

- parental income, which includes the annual earnings of both father and mother, as well as income derived from benefits, pension funds, social security benefits, interest, and dividend income

- parental expenses, which include federal, state, and social security taxes and any adjustments to income

- parental assets, which include cash, savings, and checking account balances, and the net value of all other investments (their home and farm equity may or may not be included in the calculation)

## Changes to the Formula

Determining need is quite a complicated process and one formula does not adequately address every family's situation. And while the Federal Methodology (FM) is set into law by the Congress, changes can (and often are) made to the calculation to reflect individual circumstances.

Financial aid counselors may use their professional judgment to determine whether the amount they expect from you is realistic. For example, the FM requires that the graduate aid applicant report base-year income. (Base-year income is income earned in the calendar year *prior* to the year in which you intend to go to graduate school.) But the amount you are asked to pay is computed on an income that you will no longer have if you enroll in school full time. So financial aid counselors can, at their discretion, change the income figure used in the calculation to reflect what you *expect* to earn in the calendar year in which you will be in school. For many, this makes more sense. However, not all financial aid counselors will agree that this expected earnings figure is the preferred one to use in the assessment of your financial need, and it is up to the school to make this determination.

Why would *anyone* not base aid on the expected income rather than the previous year's income? Well, for one, the information from the previous year is verifiable using tax returns; your expected income is clearly not. And second, using last year's income places the emphasis on planning ahead and saving some of the money for your schooling rather than relying on taxpayers' money and school support.

# THE APPLICATION PROCESS—AN OVERVIEW

"I spent five months gathering the forms and information necessary to apply for financial aid," says Katherine Williams, a first-year master's student at the University of Southern California. "When I was done, I told myself that no course work or research paper requirements could ever be as bad as what I had just gone through. So far, I was right."

The process by which you apply for financial aid can be lengthy and complex, with much potential for confusion or delay. Even if you previously applied for aid as an undergraduate, you may be unfamiliar with some of the specific requirements for graduate aid. In fact, the process for many students changes each year.

The bottom line is, every student, graduate *and* undergraduate, applying for federal need-based financial aid must complete the Free Application for Federal Student Aid (FAFSA) and, sometimes, a separate application form for certain loan programs. This is true regardless of how many or which graduate schools are being considered (several schools can be designated on the FAFSA).

However, hundreds of schools and private scholarship foundations also require students to complete the College Scholarship Service's (CSS) Financial Aid PROFILE, a form that is similar to the FAFSA but used only for institutional aid. Furthermore, additional applications must be completed for other types of federal aid such as the Javits and Harris Fellowships. And some schools and private foundations require their own aid applications.

Therefore, is it essential that you become familiar with the application process and that you check with the Financial Aid Office at the graduate schools to which you are applying for updated information.

## What Happens to Your Federal Application

Once the FAFSA is mailed in, the wheels of the financial aid process begin to turn. In approximately three to four weeks, the school(s) you have designated on the FAFSA will receive the information. You will also receive a confirmation that will include a summary of the data you submitted. Check carefully to make sure the information sent to the school(s) is accurate and you've correctly identified the schools you want to receive the information. If not, follow the instructions for making corrections, and make your corrections quickly and thoroughly.

Your acknowledgment, the Institutional Student Information Record (ISIR) will also show your calculated family contribution. The processor, the organization that analyzed your information, does not decide how much aid you get; it merely provides the school(s) with a calculated Expected Family Contribution. It will be up to the school itself to award the aid.

## Verifying the Information

Your school(s) will, most likely, request that you send copies of documents that support and verify the information you provided on the application. Never send your original document unless specifically requested to do so. In most cases, you will be asked for one or more of the following:

- *Income tax forms:* You may be required to provide copies of your federal income tax return for the previous year, which will be used to verify the information reported on your application. If the school requests parental income information, you may also be required to provide a copy of your parents' income tax return(s).

- *Untaxed income verification:* If you reported any untaxed income on your financial aid application, you may also be asked to provide copies of official documents supporting the figures you reported. Generally, you will have an end-of-year summary from the agency administering the program that you can send as proof.

- *Asset verification:* On occasion, a school may request documents that verify your assets. These may include bank accounts, real estate investments, and partnerships. You should be prepared to verify the asset figures you reported on your application, including the equity in your home even though it is not required for federal aid.

- *Special circumstances:* If you requested special consideration because of disability, limitation, or special need, you should be prepared to verify that information. Supporting documents may include prescriptions, doctor bills, doctor instructions, letters from appropriate agencies, etc.

*Note:* Some schools are exempt from these standard verification requirements because they participate in a project conducted by the Department of Education Institutional Quality Assurance Division. Under the project, schools complete a series of exercises and verification techniques designed to ensure that federal funds are being awarded and disbursed properly on campus. A percentage of those receiving financial aid are also randomly selected by the school to participate in the quality assurance process. The process requires review of adjusted gross income, U.S. taxes paid, social security benefits, child support, household size, number of family members in college, and untaxed income. If you are selected, you will be sent a worksheet that you must complete and return to the Financial Aid Office.

## Organizing Your Personal Financial Aid Records

1. Ultimately, *you* are responsible for seeing that your application is complete. So photocopy all papers, forms, and applications that you send to the Financial Aid Office.
2. Start your own financial aid file, and keep all your financial aid records and information in it for every year that you apply for aid. This file should include a record of all your loan obligations, promissory notes, fact sheets, truth-in-lending statements, etc.
3. Keep copies of all your tax papers (income tax return, W–2 statements) as well as savings passbooks or other papers reporting income and assets.
4. Double check all forms for accuracy and completeness. Parents', spouses', and applicant's signatures are important. If the processing center or graduate school where you mail your application receives an unsigned form, it will be returned for completion, adding several days or weeks to the application time.
5. Your full name and social security number should be clearly printed on every form, particularly on documents you included separately. If your parents and/or spouse are asked to submit letters or tax returns for completion of your application, be sure they write *your* full name in a prominent place on *each* page.
6. Respond promptly to any requests you may receive for additional information. These may come from the Admissions Office, the Financial Aid Office, the state loan-guarantee agency, or the bank.
7. Stay abreast of any current legislative activity at the state or national level that may affect your continuing eligibility to receive aid. Student financial aid programs have been subject

to many changes in recent years, making it difficult to be entirely accurate in the printing of any piece of relevant information.

Source: Elizabeth Hoffman and Nancy Stafford, *FACTS: Financial Aid for College Through Scholarships and Loans*, Wellesley, MA: Richards House, 1989.

## Students' Rights and Responsibilities

You will often hear the phrase "student rights and responsibilities" and see it written in the various financial aid guidebooks and the school's catalogs. Basically, these are tips to tell you what the school thinks are your responsibilities and what they believe are theirs. These lists are required by Consumer Protection laws written in the early 1980s. Here is one from Georgetown University's "Graduate Student Financial Aid Handbook."

*Students have the right to know:*

What the school's financial aid policy is; what forms of aid the school has available to distribute; the deadlines for applying for financial aid; what cost of attendance budget the Financial Aid Office uses to calculate aid eligibility; how financial need is determined; what portion of their aid is in the form of a loan; how much is work, and how much is an outright grant; the school's tuition refund policy; the school's financial aid appeals process; and the school's definition of satisfactory academic progress.

This list is just the basics; some schools may publish more extensive lists. Here is another example:

*Students are responsible for:*

*Meeting deadlines.* Financial aid is awarded on a first-come, first-served basis. If you apply late you may not receive the full amount of aid for which you otherwise might have been eligible.

*Recordkeeping.* You are strongly urged to keep copies of all of your university financial transactions. Copies of the following forms should be kept in your personal files: your financial aid application and worksheets, loan applications, loan promissory notes, award letters, admissions acceptance letter, tax returns, canceled checks paid to the university, and letters from the Financial Aid Office.

*Reporting changes.* Any changes in your financial aid status must be reported immediately. If you used estimated earnings on your application because you had not yet completed your tax returns, you must report actual earnings to the Financial Aid Office as soon as they are available.

To avoid jeopardizing your aid eligibility, you must respond quickly to the Financial Aid Office's request for additional or supplemental information. Changes to be reported include: any change in student, spouse, or parent (if required) income; scholarships, stipends, or loans received from any outside organization or agency; any change in your marital status and/or that of your parents (if applicable); any change in enrollment status.

*Renewing aid.* You must apply for aid each year by completing current applications. Keep in mind that financial aid is not automatically renewable each year. You must submit new applications each year.

## Awarding Aid

Once your financial need has been established, the next step is for the Financial Aid Office to put together an award package. This process is known as "packaging" because, in most instances, a combination—or package—of various financial aid programs are offered to meet your need. A sample award letter appears on p. 60.

If you are not eligible for aid, you receive a deny-aid letter. The award package is designed to meet as much of your need as possible. Naturally, all awards are contingent upon the following:

- availability of funds from federal, state, and institutional sources
- accuracy of information provided on the application
- enrollment status: if aid was packaged based on full-time enrollment and you decide to enroll for less than full time, your financial aid will be adjusted accordingly
- compliance with requests to submit additional documentation to support your application

*Note:* If you receive additional aid from an outside source that brings your total award to an amount greater than your need, your aid will be reduced dollar-for-dollar so that you are not "overawarded." The term "overaward" is used by the U.S. Department of Education to denote when students' resources exceed their needs. By reducing your aid, the federal government ensures that Federal funds are being awarded only up to the amount of your demonstrated need.

## Sample Packages

The sample awards shown in the following chart illustrate a variety of packages. They do not represent what any given student may actually be awarded. Note that "student resources" refers to the expected family contribution as calculated by the Financial Aid Office after a review of the aid applications and supporting documents. This figure may not be the actual support provided by you, your parents, or other family members. Rather, it reflects the amount of support the formula assumes is available from savings, income, and assets.

# Sample Awards

---

**Sample I**

| | |
|---|---|
| Budget | $20,900 |
| Student Resources | −9,500 |
| | |
| Financial Aid Eligibility | $11,400 |
| Your Aid Package: | |
| Federal Subsidized Stafford or Direct Loan | $ 8,500 |
| Federal Work-Study | 2,000 |
| Federal Perkins Loan | 900 |
| | |
| Total Aid | $11,400 |
| Unmet Need | 0 |

---

**Sample II**

| | |
|---|---|
| Budget | $29,090 |
| Student Resources | −10,590 |
| | |
| Financial Aid Eligibility | $18,500 |
| Your Aid Package: | |
| Federal Subsidized Stafford or Direct Loan | $ 8,500 |
| Federal Unsubsidized Stafford or Direct Loan | 10,000 |
| | |
| Total Aid | $18,500 |
| Unmet Need | 0 |

---

**Sample III**

| | |
|---|---|
| Budget | $29,090 |
| Student Resources | −7,400 |
| | |
| Financial Aid Eligibility | $21,690 |
| Your Aid Package: | |
| Academic Department Grant | $10,000 |
| Federal Subsidized Stafford or Direct Loan | −8,500 |
| | |
| Total Aid | $18,500 |
| Unmet Need | $ 3,190 |

You will notice that in one of the samples there is what is called "unmet need." This is a term that financial aid counselors use when they recognize that you *need* the funds to complete your financial aid package but they have no more funds to offer. Many graduate schools have financial aid packages that contain an amount of unmet need. (Sometimes this phenomenon is called "gapping.") Whatever way you look at it, it is money that you must find somewhere else. You can either reduce your cost of attendance by cutting your expenses somehow or find alternative funding programs, like the Federal Unsubsidized Stafford or private loan programs discussed in Chapters 3 and 4 to fill this gap in your financial aid package.

## Refunds

If you withdraw from school and have received aid, the school must have a policy to refund any part of the tuition, fees, room and board, and other charges owed to you. First, most schools require that you put your request for withdrawal in writing. Second, refund policies vary among schools. Some, for example, refund a portion of the amount paid if you withdraw prior to the end of the fourth week of classes. To participate in federal financial aid programs, an institution must have a fair and equitable refund policy consistent with specific standards approved by the institution's nationally recognized accrediting agency and the U.S. Department of Education. State laws also may affect a school's refund policy. The policy must be provided in writing to prospective students prior to their enrollment and also must be made known to currently enrolled students. Consult a financial aid counselor for the most recent information on refund policies at your school.

# U.S. TAX ISSUES

As a graduate student, you should pay close attention to the tax laws that affect the financial support you receive. The basic rules are (1) the amount of grant aid you receive that is greater than your tuition is taxable; (2) all forms of work and service-related fellowships are taxable; and (3) loans are not taxable.

# Sample Financial Aid Award Letter

Student ID# _____

Status _____

Academic Year _____

Date _____

Dear Graduate Student:

The Office of Financial Aid is pleased to offer you the following financial aid for the 1996-97 academic year.

Please sign and return the white copy of this award offering by _____. Replies not received by this date will result in your award being revoked. You must accept (ACC) or reject (REJ) each item offered, indicating your decision by a check mark in the appropriate column.

| Type of Aid | First Semester | Second Semester | Total | ACC | REJ |
| --- | --- | --- | --- | --- | --- |
| Trustee's Scholarship | $1000 | $1000 | $2000 | | |
| Federal Stafford Loan | $4250 | $4250 | $8500 | | |
| Federal Perkins Loan | $2500 | $2500 | $5000 | | |
| Total Aid Awarded | $7750 | $7750 | $15,500 | | |

Awards from all programs are contingent upon actual funding levels.

Comments:_____

Status: Signifies the enrollment/attendance status on which this award is made. A change in attendance status will result in a revised award.

### Acceptance/Relinquishment

❏ I accept the aid offered above. I have read and signed the Statement of Educational Purpose on the reverse side. I understand that this offer is not official until copies of my current tax returns or other income verification are received and reviewed by the Financial Aid Office.

❏ I do not accept this award and hereby relinquish these funds.

### Awards Not Mentioned

❏ I have received _____ from _____.

❏ I have not received any additional awards, but will notify the Financial Aid Office in writing if I do.

The 1986 Tax Reform Act changed previous tax treatment of scholarships and fellowships. Subsequent changes to the tax law in the form of amendments to the Tax Reform Act of 1986 and the Technical and Miscellaneous Revenue Amendments of 1988 modified the tax treatment of scholarships and fellowships with particular respect to graduate students who perform services such as graduate teaching or have research assistantships. Taken together, these changes in tax law have resulted in a national definition, for federal tax purposes, of components of scholarships, fellowships, and assistantships.

Stipends, either as the component of fellowships provided as a living allowance or as the component of research or teaching assistantships that represent compensation for services, are considered taxable income to the student. The 1986 Tax Reform Act made a distinction between those stipends and the component of the scholarship, fellowship, or assistantship that represents payment of tuition, fees, books, or equipment required for a degree program.

Institutional discretion is permitted in setting the level of each component within these categories. Required books and equipment should be well documented by the institution, and you should keep receipts of the purchase of these items. Such books and equipment must be required of all students in a given academic program.

Your school, and in many instances your academic department, makes the determination to provide tuition reductions or tuition waivers to teaching and research assistants as part of the conditions of appointment. For graduate students performing teaching or research services, these reductions and waivers are considered qualified scholarships and thus can be excluded from income (i.e., they are tax free) by a provision in Section 117(d)(5) of the Internal Revenue Code.

The general rule for the qualified tuition reductions under Section 117(d)(5), as amended by the 1988 Act, allows graduate teaching and research assistants to exclude from income amounts received from their universities as tuition coverage.

The regulations specifically require educational organizations to determine which part of their tuition or tuition reduction is allowable for payment for services. In other words, universities must determine which part of the tuition reduction does not represent payment for services and, therefore, may be excluded from income.

The Tax Reform Act also specifies that nondegree students who receive tuition remission may no longer exclude the dollar amount of the tuition remission from taxable income.

## Non-U.S. Citizens/Non-U.S. Residents

Graduate students who are not U.S. citizens or permanent residents of the United States are subject to different and often more stringent tax regulations. This tax treatment will vary depending on the country of origin because of the tax treaty status between the United States and other nations. U.S. source income is subject to withholding at a tax rate from 14 percent to 30 percent depending on visa status, with F, J, and M visas subject to the lowest rate providing the individual is a degree candidate. Non-U.S. source income is subject to different tax regulations. In general, non-U.S. residents should be familiar with the tax treaty status of their countries of residence and the tax status of non-U.S. source income with respect to funds used or earned for the payment of tuition, fees, and living allowances. Tax treaties are summarized in IRS Publication 515, "Withholding of Tax on Nonresident Aliens and Foreign Corporations," which is available free of charge by writing to the Forms Distribution Center, IRS, P.O. Box 25866, Richmond, Virginia, 23289.

## Employee Benefits

Many employers, including colleges and universities, offer employer-sponsored educational assistance benefits under Section 127 of the IRS Code. College and university employees who are not TA's or RA's still may find such benefits useful.

Again, the basic rule is that benefits received for enrolling in graduate courses by persons holding a bachelor's degree are taxable.

As this book went to press, Congress was debating whether to reinstate the employee benefit legislation that expired. This old legislation taxed any benefits exceeding $5,250. As of now, *all* employee benefits are considered taxable income. IRS regulations do not require employers to issue 1099 forms for fellowship or scholarship support. But they do require individual taxpayers (including students) to report any earned income from stipends or living allowances.

You should contact your school's personnel department to find out the status of employee benefits. And for more information, refer to the IRS issued Publication 520 which discusses in detail individual reporting requirements and reflects the latest changes in tax forms and filing requirements.

# FEDERAL
# AND
# STATE
# AID

**3**

"**W**hen I was researching financial aid," says Gloria Taylor, a Minneapolis-based engineer who financed her graduate education through a combination of federal loans and Federal Work-Study assistance, "I assumed there wouldn't be much for me, that everything was geared totally toward undergraduates. Fortunately, I was wrong."

## FEDERAL FINANCIAL AID

At the graduate level, most federal financial aid awards are in the form of loans, with a sprinkling of grants and service-related programs depending upon your field of study. Federal student aid is part of the Higher Education Act, which is divided into many titles. The main financial aid programs are found in Title IV. In addition to Title IV, graduate students receive money through Title VI, International Education, and Title IX, Graduate Education. Because of the political nature of federal and state financial aid programs, be sure to check with the Financial Aid Office at the school in which you intend to enroll for any late-breaking changes.

If you're a novice in the quest for financial aid, the first thing for you to know is that the U. S. government participates in the funding of graduate students through *many* different agencies as well as through the Department of Education. It provides over $200 million in graduate student support through departments such as the National Institutes of Health, the National Science Foundation, the National Aeronautics and Space Administration, the U.S. Information Agency, and the Departments of Agriculture, Defense, and Energy.

The amounts and types of grant assistance vary considerably, as do application procedures and deadline dates. Some are specifically designated scholarship programs such as the Jacob Javits and the Patricia Roberts Harris Fellowship Programs. Some, like the National Science Foundation or the National Institutes of Health grants, are research monies awarded to government institutions that include within them financial support for students.

# FEDERAL GOVERNMENT GRANTS

As a graduate student applying for financial aid, you would like, I am sure, the bulk of your award package to be in the form of outright scholarships or grants because such money doesn't have to be repaid later. Of course, this isn't always possible, but there is some grant money out there, some of which may be available to you.

## Qualifying for Federal Title IV Money

More than 8,000 colleges and universities take part in the U.S. government's Title IV financial aid programs. To qualify for this federal money—which can be used only for expenses related to attending school—you must first meet the following requirements. You must be:

- enrolled at least half-time (6 semester hours)
- a U.S. citizen or an eligible noncitizen
- making satisfactory progress in your course of study
- neither in default, nor owing a refund for any federal aid you have received in the past

For specific questions regarding Title IV federal financial aid programs, you can call the Federal Student Aid Information Center 1-800-4FEDAID, which can help with:

- checking on whether a school participates in federal aid programs
- explaining student eligibility requirements
- explaining the process by which financial aid awards are determined
- channeling your complaints to the right office
- explaining the verification process (the Department of Education or your school may require you to prove that what you reported on your application is correct)
- mailing publications

If you are hearing impaired, you may call 1-800-730-8913, a TDD number at the Information Center, for help with any federal student aid questions. Be sure to tell them that you are interested in funds for graduate education. The bulk of their calls are from undergraduates. The Information Center cannot help you if you are calling to find out whether your application has been processed.

## Title IX Programs

In 1986 Title IX—graduate programs—was expanded, and the 1992 reauthorization of the Higher Education Act made additional changes. The education amendments that will be made in 1997 and 1998 may well change these programs again. The current mood is to consolidate these programs into one or two categories. The purpose of Title IX is to foster and support graduate and professional education to provide incentives and support for U.S. citizens to complete doctoral degree programs leading to academic careers, especially women and students from underrepresented groups. It provides support for students from underrepresented groups to complete master's and professional degree programs. Title IX funds cannot be awarded for study at a school or department of divinity.

Like many federal programs, the status of Title IX fellowships is uncertain and there may be significant cuts in the funding levels of these programs. You should check with the graduate school Financial Aid Office for the latest information about Title IX funding.

Title IX includes the following programs:

### Grants to Institutions and Consortia to Encourage Women and Minority Participation in Graduate Education

These grants are made to schools to help them identify talented undergraduates who demonstrate financial need. With this grant, minority students and women have an opportunity to prepare for graduate fields in which they traditionally have been underrepresented.

### Patricia Roberts Harris Fellowship Program

These fellowships are awarded to schools to distribute to master's- and doctoral-level minority graduate students and women underrepresented in graduate fields. Fifty percent of the funds must be awarded to schools for master's and professional study, and fifty percent of the funds must be awarded for fellowships for doctoral study. Awarding priority is given to minority students and women pursuing master's-level study leading to careers in the public interest and to those entering doctoral study, particularly in the fields of mathematics and science.

For each fellowship recipient, schools will receive $9000 toward the cost of tuition. The school must then provide the recipient with the difference between $9000 and the actual tuition charged. In addition, there is a $14,900 stipend for other educational expenses. Awards are available for a maximum of three years provided you are making satisfactory academic progress.

### Fellowships in Areas of National Need

The National Need Fellowship Program has been in existence since 1988. Its purpose is to offer financial assistance to students enrolled in specific programs for which there is both a national need and a lack of qualified personnel. The annual definition of "national need" is determined by the U.S. Secretary of Education in consultation with other federal agencies as well as with nonprofit organizations concerned with doctoral education. Current areas include chemistry, engineering, mathematics, physics, and area studies. For students in good standing, fellowships may be renewed for a total of three years.

Grants are made to institutions, which, in turn, award students. The amount a student receives is based on demonstrated financial need using the Federal Methodology of need analysis. National Need Fellowships are mainly designed to promote teaching and research and are awarded only to graduate students of superior ability. Recipients must be U.S. citizens or permanent residents (or in the process of becoming such).

Participating schools apply directly to the Department of Education, which awards funds competitively to institutions for three-year traineeships in doctoral programs. Students are selected by the school that must then confirm that awardees have financial need, excellent academic records, and plans for careers involving either teaching or research. Application deadlines are usually mid-January for new awards and early April for continuing awards.

Contact the Financial Aid Office or the Graduate Dean's Office of your school to see whether it participates in this fellowship program.

### Faculty Development Fellowship Program

The Faculty Development Fellowship Program, created as part of the 1992 amendments to the Higher Education Act, enables schools to assist talented faculty and members of underrepresented groups in obtaining a doctoral degree. Priority will be given to schools that provide fellowship recipients with tuition waivers, a minimum $2000 stipend, *or* additional financial support in conjunction with teaching or research activities. Schools that receive these funds must ensure that the fellowship recipients will teach at an institution of higher education where minority undergraduates are likely to benefit from the educational experience and academic achievement of the recipient. The stipend level can not exceed $14,000 per year, depending on the student's demonstrated financial need. One year of teaching is required for each year of assistance. Otherwise, students must repay part or all of the fellowship received plus interest.

**Assistance for Training in the Legal Profession**
This federal grant is given directly to the Council of Legal Education Opportunity (CLEO) to carry out a program to assist minority, low-income, or educationally disadvantaged graduates in the legal profession. Funds are used for counseling applicants to assist them in gaining admission to accredited law schools; for a six-week intensive summer program designed to prepare minority, low-income, and educationally disadvantaged individuals for the successful completion of legal studies; and/or for an academic year of tutorial services, academic advice, and counseling designed to assist eligible participants success-fully to complete their legal training.

Contact the law school you wish to attend to determine if they participate in the CLEO program on the Law School Clinical Experience Program.

**Law School Clinical Experience Program**
The purpose of this program is to provide law schools with assistance, through grants and contracts, to continue, expand, or establish programs providing clinical law experience.

# Other Federal Grant Programs

In addition to Title IX money, there are several other federal grant programs of which you should be aware. They are described below.

**National Science Foundation Fellowships (NSF)**
The goal of this program is to improve the human resource base of science and engineering in the United States. Fellowships are available as well for women in engineering and for minority students in science and engineering. For students in good standing, awards are for three years of graduate study.

Fellows receive $8600 toward the cost of tuition and required fees (the institution must pay the remaining tuition in the form of a grant). The annual stipend is $14,400 plus a $1000 travel allowance. This fellowship is for students studying in engineering, natural sciences, social sciences, and the history and philosophy of science. U.S. citizens or permanent residents of the United States are eligible to apply. Applicants must not have completed more than 20 semester hours, 30 quarter hours, or the equivalent. The application deadline is generally the first week in November and awards are announced in mid-March.

*Contact:* NSF Graduate Research Fellowship Program
Oak Ridge Associated Universities
P.O. Box 3010
Oak Ridge, TN 37831-3010
423-241-4300

### Federal Scholarship for Students with Exceptional Financial Need (EFN)

This program is available to medical students who demonstrate exceptional financial need. Federal regulations define exceptional financial need as personal and family resources of $6700 or less as determined by a standard method of need analysis. Applicants must supply parents' income and asset information regardless of their age, marital, or financial status. Most medical schools will automatically consider you for EFN if you apply for financial aid. The amount of EFN awarded is determined by the Financial Aid Office.

*Contact:* Check with your school's financial aid counselor for more information.

### Financial Assistance for Disadvantaged Health Professions Students (FADHPS)

This award is also for students with exceptional financial need, as determined by a standard method of need analysis. FADHPS awards are renewable. Most medical schools will automatically consider you for FADHPS when you apply for financial aid.

*Contact:* Check with your school's financial aid counselor for more information.

### Department of Health and Human Services (HHS), National Institutes of Health (NIH)—Professional Nurse Traineeship Program

This is a portable award covering all or part of tuition and fees as well as stipends of up to $6552 per year. U.S. citizens or permanent residents who are currently licensed as professional nurses and enrolled in master's or doctoral programs are eligible. Application procedures vary. Check with your financial aid officer or the contact person listed below.

*Contact:* Dean of Nursing Program at an eligible institution.

### Department of Health and Human Services (HHS), National Institutes of Health (NIH)—Public Health Service Commission Corps (COSTEP)

Technically, this is a service-related award, since awardees receive financial assistance in return for the work they perform. The Public Health Service (PHS) offers students in medicine, nursing, pharmacy, and other health professions the chance to gain professional experience at sites around the country through programs called COSTEP, the Commissioned Officer Student Training and Extern Program. COSTEP participants work in the office of the assistant secretary for health; in one of the eight PHS agencies, such as the Health Care Policy and Research Agency; or in other federal programs staffed by PHS health professionals, such as the Environmental Protection Agency.

This award consists of full pay (to equal $1950 monthly for a single person) for an assistant junior health service officer, who is also eligible for medical and dental care while on duty. Applicants must have completed at least one year of study in medical, dental, or veterinary school, or be enrolled in a graduate program in another health-related field. The student must not be a member of, nor owe a service obligation to, another uniformed service.

Deadlines for COSTEP applications are December 31 for positions May 1 through August 31, May 1 for positions September 1 through December 31, and October 1 for positions January 1 through April 30.

*Contact:* COSTEP
PHS Recruitment
Suite 600
201 Greensboro Drive
McLean, VA 22102
301-594-2919 or 800-221-9393 (toll-free)

### Department of Health and Human Services (HHS), National Institutes of Health (NIH)—Program of Financial Assistance for Disadvantaged Health Professionals

The award covers costs of attendance that are unmet through other sources of financial aid or $10,000, whichever is less. Monies can be used toward tuition or other reasonable educational expenses. Students from disadvantaged backgrounds with exceptional financial need and enrolled full time in a dentistry, medicine, or osteopathic program are eligible.

Application procedures vary. Contact the financial aid counselor at your school or the contact listed here.

*Contact:* Health Resources and Services Administration
Bureau of Health Professions, Division of Student Assistance
Parklawn Building, Room 8–34
5600 Fishers Lane
Rockville, MD 20857
301-443-5798

### National Health Service Corps (NHSC)

The award covers tuition and a monthly stipend of $796 plus books and related educational expenses and health insurance if the school requires it. There is a minimum federal service obligation of two years for each year a student receives an NHSC scholarship. Full-time practitioners will meet their obligations by working in areas in the U.S. designated as Health Manpower Shortage Areas. About 400 awards are made each year to U.S. citizens enrolled in full-time health-professions school. The application deadline is the last Friday in March.

Application procedures vary. Contact your financial aid counselor or the contact listed here.

*Contact:* National Health Service Corps Scholarship Program
Suite 1200
1010 Wayne Avenue
Silver Spring, MD 20910
800-638-0824 (toll-free)

### National Institutes of Health (NIH) Training Grants

Academic departments apply directly to NIH for training grants that usually provide the full amount of tuition and fees plus a stipend of $8500 paid over a twelve-month period. If the source of the award is a National Institutes of Health Training Grant funded through the National Research Service Award (NRSA) Act of 1974, it is expected that following NRSA funding you will serve in one of the fields of teaching or research (including basic research in pharmaceutical and chemical industries) or an approved alternate service for a period usually as long as the duration of the traineeship. Trainees who do not work in approved fields are required to pay back the amount of the stipend received. Appointments may be made for a period of no less than nine months. In addition, NIH administers a minority fellowship program called the Minority Access to Research Careers (MARC) National Institute of General Sciences Predoctoral Fellowships Program.

You must be enrolled in a graduate program in a health-related field. Application procedures vary.

*Contact:* Your academic department or:
Division of Research and Training Grants
National Institutes of Health
Room 449 Westwood Building
533 Westbard Avenue
Bethesda, MD 20857

## National Aeronautics and Space Administration (NASA)— Graduate Student Researchers Program

This program awards grants to graduate students whose research is compatible with NASA research programs. Awardees are selected each year based on a competitive evaluation of academic qualifications, the proposed research plan or plan of study, and, where appropriate, the planned utilization of NASA research facilities. Fellowships are for one year and are renewable for up to three years, based on progress and evaluation reports. Approximately 100 new awards are made each year.

You must be a U.S. citizen and enrolled in a graduate program in an area compatible with current NASA research projects. Check with the address listed below for further information. Students may enter the program any time during their graduate work or may apply prior to receiving their baccalaureate degrees. The application deadline is February 1; awards are made by spring.

*Contact:* John T. Lynch
National Aeronautics and Space Administration Headquarters
Washington, D.C. 20546
202-358-1530

## National Space Grant College and Fellowship Program

In 1987, Congress authorized the National Space Grant College and Fellowships Program to help maintain U.S. capabilities in aerospace and technology through a national network of universities, industry, and federal, state, and local governments. The program includes:

- designated space-grant college/consortia that will provide leadership for a national network on universities and colleges

- awards to support space-grant programs at other institutions that will expand university participation in aerospace fields
- space-grant fellowships

All states have become participating members of the space grant state consortia. Application procedures vary by state. Check with NASA for eligibility requirements, applications, and award notification dates.

*Contact:* Campus coordinator at your school. Information is also available on the Internet.

## Global Change Research Fellowships

The purpose of Global Change Research Fellowships is to ensure a continued supply of highly qualified scientists to support rapid growth in the study of earth as a system. Over 250 fellowships have been awarded since the inception of the program in 1990 and up to fifty new fellowships are awarded each year, subject to availability of funds. The fellowship is renewable for an additional two years, pending satisfactory progress.

The awards are for $20,000, with an additional $2000 available to your faculty adviser to help provide support for your research. Students pursuing Ph.D.'s in aspects of global change research are eligible, provided that the specific research topic is relevant to NASA's global change research efforts. A brochure describing these programs will be made available upon written request to the contact listed below. Applications must be received by March 15; awards are announced on June 30.

*Contact:* NASA Global Change Fellowship Program
Code YSP-44
NASA Headquarters
Washington, D.C. 20546
*Program Information:*
Global Change Fellowship Program
Code YS
Office of Mission to Planet Earth
NASA Headquarters
Washington, D.C. 20546

## NASA Graduate Cooperative Education Program

The Graduate Cooperative Education Program is tailored to the individual student and is usually designed around a series of work experiences. These work intervals may be in one work area or encompass various work experiences. At present, all work experiences are at the NASA Langley Research Center in Hampton, Virginia. Permanent positions may be available after graduation; however, due to budget constraints, hiring will be limited.

Full-time graduate students in areas related to science and space are eligible. Application deadlines vary. Interested applicants should contact NASA directly to discuss the deadlines at the various locations.

*Contact:* Libby Wyatt
Personnel Office
NASA
400 Maryland Avenue, SW
Washington, D.C. 20546
202-358-1575

### National Research Council—Graduate Research Award Program on Public-Sector Aviation Issues

The Graduate Research Award Program aims to stimulate thought and to support research in public-sector aviation issues among the future managers and policy makers in the area. A stipend is awarded during the various stages of assembling a research paper on a subject chosen by the candidate, but within the purview of the program. Successful applicants receive a stipend of $6000 for the Graduate Research Award Program for a research paper on a subject chosen from within the program's purpose. Progress payments will be made during the research, with final payment on completion and acceptance of the paper. The award is offered only to citizens and permanent residents of the United States. Students must be enrolled in a master's or doctoral program at an accredited institution.

Applicants are judged on academic qualifications, career goals, and proposed research. Application deadlines are generally in early October; award recipients are announced in December.

*Contact:* Graduate Research Award Program
Room GR-326E
Transportation Research Board
National Research Council
2101 Constitution Avenue, NW
Washington, D.C. 20418
800-424-9818 ext. 3206 (toll-free)

### U.S. Department of Energy Professional Internship Program

The program is designed to provide educational research training in a variety of disciplines and technologies for beginning graduate students seeking advanced degrees. Assignments afford trainees the opportunity to apply and practice the theories and principles learned in the classroom. During the appointment period, the award pays trainees monthly stipends of $1300 to $1400. Applicants must be graduate students who have not yet begun their theses or dissertations. Applicants must also be U.S. citizens who are enrolled full time in a master's or doctoral degree program in energy-related disciplines. Applications are accepted quarterly. For exact dates, contact the person listed below.

*Contact:* Betty Brewster
Professional Internship Program
U.S. Department of Energy
Oak Ridge, TN 37831-0117
615-576-3427

### U.S. Department of Justice, National Institute of Justice (NIJ)
### Assistant Attorney General's Graduate Research Fellowships

The purpose of the Graduate Research Fellowship Program is to support research that enhances the capabilities of law enforcement and criminal justice to combat crime and substance abuse. The fellowship offers graduate students an opportunity to conduct independent research on relevant policy and practice issues in criminal justice. Awards are preferably for one year or less, although awards for up to eighteen months are considered. Four to six highly competitive awards are made each year.

Advanced doctoral students can be awarded as much as $35,000 to support their research. The basic stipend is $10,000 for twelve months; the award may include certain university fees, an allowance for dependents, supplies, computer time, travel, etc. Smaller awards are available for master's degree students whose proposed research projects are of outstanding quality and have relevance to criminal justice policy and practical issues.

Application deadlines are April 15, August 15, September 15, and December 15. Applicants are encouraged to contact the NIJ to discuss topic viability and proposed content before submitting proposals.

*Contact:* Dr. Kevin Jack Riley
Assistant Attorney General's Graduate
Research Fellowship Program
National Institute of Justice
633 Indiana Avenue, NW, Room 866
Washington, D.C. 20531
202-616-9030

# FEDERAL LOANS

Despite the number of fellowships and grants just listed, unfortunately, much of the financial aid for graduate students is in the form of loans. "As an undergraduate, I did everything I could to avoid borrowing money," says Cathy Chavez, a second-year engineering student. "But if you're not lucky enough to have a lot of money or come from a family that does, then you have to resign yourself to the reality that graduate school means taking out loans."

A recent Congressional report found that more than two-thirds of all students leave graduate school with debt. Those who attend public graduate schools on the average owe about $8000 upon receiving their degrees, while those attending private graduate schools owe more along the lines of $12,000. This average also includes all those graduate students who did not borrow anything either as an undergraduate *or* a graduate student. Of those who did borrow, the average amount they borrowed was significantly higher and, in fact, from the mid-1970s to the late 1980s, grant and scholarship awards decreased by one-third while loan awards increased fourfold.

But borrowing for graduate school is an investment in your future. Investments generally involve taking a sum of money, placing it in a financial vehicle, and sometime later reaping the rewards. In a sense, going to graduate school can be thought of in the same way, in that your earning power will increase substantially with a graduate degree.

The average starting salary for someone with just an undergraduate degree is about $23,000. Adding in as much as 10 percent for both cost-of-living and merit increases in salary, the average total earnings over a four-year period would be about $107,000. By comparison, the average starting salary for someone holding a graduate degree is $28,000, or 20 percent more. Adding in the same 10 percent salary increases, the average earnings over a four-year period would be about $130,000. The difference between the undergraduate and the graduate's earning power after four years is $23,000—enough to cover a substantial part of a graduate degree program. Similarly, the $20,000 in loans taken out for a graduate degree could be repaid fully in four years simply from the higher salaries paid to those with graduate degrees. Measured in terms of earning capacity, then, graduate school is clearly a good investment.

With that in mind, consider the following loan programs now available from the federal government. You can also refer to the charts on pages 81–83.

## Federal Stafford Loan Program

The Guaranteed Student Loan, renamed the Federal Stafford Student Loan Program (after Senator Robert T. Stafford) is the largest source of financial aid for graduate study. There are two different loans under this program, the Subsidized Stafford Student Loan and the Unsubsidized Stafford Student Loan. The difference is that the subsidized loan is based on need while the unsubsidized program is not. Also, interest does not accrue on the subsidized program until six months after you leave school while interest begins to accrue on the unsubsidized program sixty days after you receive the loan. To qualify for either loan you must be a U.S. citizen or permanent resident of the United States, be enrolled at least half time in a degree or certificate program, and be making satisfactory academic progress. Federal Stafford Student Loans are administered through banks, credit unions, or other lending institutions.

Graduate students may borrow a maximum of $8,500 per year from the subsidized Stafford Student Loan program, up to a total of $65,500, and $10,000 per year from the unsubsidized Stafford Student Loan, up to a total of $138,500. The interest rate on Federal Stafford Student Loans is variable and tied to the 91-day Treasury Bill. The maximum rate is 8.25 percent and the rate through June 1997 is 7.66 percent.

To qualify for a Subsidized Federal Stafford Student Loan, you must demonstrate financial need as determined by the Federal Methodology of need analysis described in Chapter 2. Federal Stafford Student Loans are generally disbursed in two parts, in fall and in spring. When the loan is disbursed, a nonrefundable insurance premium of up to 3 percent (varies by state) is deducted from your loan proceeds as well as a 1 percent origination fee. No cosigner is necessary since these loans are not based upon creditworthiness. All borrowers must attend loan entrance and exit interviews in which their rights and obligations are explained.

Federal Stafford Loan repayment begins after a six-month grace period following your date of last enrollment as at least a half-time student. You have ten years in which to repay these loans. A $50 minimum monthly payment is required. There is no penalty for prepayment. The tables in Chapter 1 show monthly and annual repayment amounts as well as percentage of salary required to repay a loan.

To apply for a Federal Stafford Student Loan, you must complete the FAFSA and a supplemental loan application on which you specify the lender from which you will borrow. You are free to choose whichever lending institution you want, but sometimes schools have arrangements with certain lenders that could make your life easier when it comes time for loan repayment so you might want to discuss it with the Financial Aid Office.

## Federal Direct Loans

Some schools participate in the Federal Direct Loan Programs instead of the Federal Stafford Loan Programs. There are subsidized and unsubsidized Federal Direct Loans and the terms of the direct loans are virtually the same as their Stafford counterparts. You should consult the school for details about the loan program in which they participate.

## Federal Perkins Loans

Formerly the National Direct Student Loan, a Federal Perkins Loan is a low-interest loan (5 percent) available to both undergraduate and graduate students. The school is your lender, and this loan must be repaid to the school or its agent. Graduate students may borrow up to $5000 per year, to a maximum of $30,000. This total includes any Federal Perkins Loan money borrowed previously while you were in undergraduate or other graduate programs.

To qualify for a Federal Perkins Loan, you must be a U.S. citizen or permanent resident, enrolled at least half time, maintain satisfactory academic progress, and demonstrate financial need as determined by the Federal Methodology of need analysis described in Chapter 2. Federal Perkins Loans are awarded by schools to those who demonstrate the greatest financial need. Your eligibility is determined from the information you provide on your financial aid applications, and it is up to the school to determine who gets these loans.

As with the Federal Stafford and Direct Loan Programs, Federal Perkins Loan borrowers must attend entrance and exit interviews for each awarding period (explained later in this chapter). You have ten years to repay after you graduate, leave school, or drop below half-time enrollment. There is also a nine-month grace period before repayment begins, but when the grace period expires, repayment is due monthly or quarterly, with a minimum payment of $50. There is no penalty for prepayment. The tables in Chapter 1 show monthly and annual repayment amounts as well as percentage of salary required to comfortably repay a loan.

Federal Perkins Loan repayment can be deferred for specified periods of time for borrowers who meet certain conditions. They are:

- enrollment in an institution of higher education on at least a half-time basis

- service in the military, Commissioned Corps of the Public Health Service, or National Oceanic and Atmospheric Administration Corps

- volunteer service in the Peace Corps or under the Domestic Service Act of 1973 (ACTION programs) or for a tax-exempt organization if the service is comparable to Peace Corps or ACTION

- temporary total disability or care for temporarily totally disabled spouse

- serving a required internship

- parental leave

- mother of preschool children entering or reentering the work-force at a low pay rate

- conditions of hardship to the borrower (at the discretion of the school)

Some of these deferments carry very specific conditions that must be met, and all carry a length limit. Under other, more limited conditions, repayment of Federal Perkins Loans may be partially or completely canceled. They are:

- teaching in schools designated as serving low-income students

- teaching handicapped children

- service in a Head Start program

- military duty in a designated area of hostilities

- service as a law enforcement or corrections officer

- permanent total disability

- death

For further information about Federal Perkins Loans, contact the Financial Aid Office of the school you plan to attend to determine if they use any of their Federal Perkins Loan funding for graduate students.

## Loan Programs Administered by the U.S. Department of Health and Human Services (HHS)

In addition to the Federal Perkins, Federal Stafford, and Federal Direct Loan Programs that are all managed by the Department of Education, there are other need-based programs that provide assistance to future health-care practitioners. These programs are managed by the U.S. Department of Health and Human Services. They are:

- Primary Care Loan Program (PCL)
- Health Education Assistance Loan (HEAL)
- Nursing Student Loans (NSL)

**Primary Care Loan Program (PCL)**

Full-time graduate students in the health professions, health administration, clinical psychology, or public health can borrow through this revolving loan fund, in which new federal capital is periodically provided to schools by HHS. These funds are combined with the annual repayments of previous borrowers to provide funding for the neediest graduate students. Recipients must have exceptional financial need; that is, they must have resources of less than $6700 (including resources from parents and spouse) as determined by the Federal Methodology. The law requires you to provide your parents' and spouse's income and asset information, regardless of your age or marital status. Although the federal regulations provide for a maximum annual award of as much tuition plus $2500, most schools do not have sufficient PCL funds to provide any one student with such a large award.

Awards are made by the Financial Aid Office. Applicants must be U.S. citizens or permanent residents of the United States, must be making satisfactory academic progress, and must not be in default on any other government loans. The interest rate is 5 percent and no interest accrues while you are in school. You have a grace period of one year after you leave school before interest begins to accrue or before you must begin repayment. PCL loans are repayable over a ten-year period. Deferments are also available for internships and residencies. The rules governing deferments are changing as this book goes to press. In some cases the federal government may cancel or forgive your Primary Care Loan, and you should consult your school for details. This loan may not be consolidated as part of a Federal Consolidation Loan under the Higher Education Act of 1965.

**Health Education Assistance Loan Program (HEAL)**

The Health Education Assistance Loan (HEAL) is a federal program offered to students at market interest rates. The government does not provide an interest subsidy as it does with many of its other student loan programs. Like the Federal Stafford Student Loan, private banks are most often the lender. Applicants must be U.S. citizens or permanent residents of the United States, be making satisfactory academic progress, and must not be in default on any other government loans. You may borrow up to $20,000 per year, not to exceed a maximum of $80,000. The interest rate is variable and is set quarterly. The rate is determined by adding a maximum of 3 percent to the 91-day Treasury Bill rate. Interest rates, therefore, vary from 7 percent to 12 percent. An insurance fee of 8 percent is deducted from the proceeds of each loan.

To qualify for a HEAL loan, you must demonstrate financial need by filing the FAFSA. In addition, there is a separate application for HEAL, which you may get from your Financial Aid Office or from the lender. Applicants must be creditworthy, that is, they cannot have a negative credit history. Repayment begins nine months after you cease to be a full-time student at a HEAL school. HEAL borrowers have up to twenty-five years to repay their debts from this program. Graduated payments are permitted, and there is no penalty for prepayment. There are some consolidation arrangements available for HEAL borrowers. Deferments are available, and there is a cancellation provision for permanent disability. As this book goes to print Congress is debating the future of the HEAL loan. Check with your Financial Aid Office to determine whether this program is still available.

**Nursing Student Loans (NSL)**
Accredited schools of nursing are eligible to apply for these loans, and funds may be used for graduate students. The maximum amount students may borrow is $4000. The total for all years is $13,000. Interest is 5 percent; loans are repayable over a ten-year period, beginning nine months after students leave school. For more information, contact the Financial Aid Office.

## Loan Comparison Chart

### Federal Subsidized Stafford or Direct Loan

| | |
|---|---|
| Annual Loan Limit | Current law = $8,500 |
| Cumulative Loan Limit | Current law = $65,500 |
| Variable Interest Rate | 0% in school; 91-day T-Bill rate plus 2.5% while not in school |
| Need-Based Aid | Yes |
| Application Fee | None |
| Creditworthiness Test | No |
| Origination or Guarantee Fee | 4% |
| Form of Disbursement | Wired or check to the school depending on the lender |
| Deferments | No repayment while in school, some deferments after graduation |
| Prepayment Penalty | No |
| Grace Period | Six months |
| Minimum Monthly Payment | $50 |
| Length of Repayment | Up to ten years; can consolidate |

### Federal Unsubsidized Stafford or Direct Loan

| | |
|---|---|
| Annual Loan Limit | $18,500 |
| Cumulative Loan Limit | $138,500 |
| Variable Interest Rate | Ninety-One-day T-Bill rate plus 2.5% |
| Need-Based Aid | No |
| Application Fee | None |
| Creditworthiness Test | No |
| Origination or Guarantee Fee | 4% |
| Form of Disbursement | Wired or check sent to the school, depending on lender |
| Deferments | No repayment while in school, some deferments after graduation |
| Prepayment Penalty | No |
| Grace Period | Six months |
| Minimum Monthly Payment | $50 |
| Length of Repayment | Up to ten years |

### Federal Perkins Loan

| | |
|---|---|
| Annual Loan Limit | $5000 |
| Cumulative Loan Limit | $30,000 |
| Annual Interest Rate | 0% in school; 5% in repayment |
| Variable Interest Rate | NA |
| Need-Based Aid | Yes |
| Application Fee | None |
| Creditworthiness Test | No |
| Origination Fee | None |
| Guarantee Fee | None |
| Form of Disbursement | Credited to student's account or paid to student directly |
| Deferments | No repayment while in school, some deferments after graduation |
| Prepayment Penalty | No |
| Grace Period | Nine months; Six months for old National Direct Student Loans |
| Minimum Monthly Payment | $40 |
| Length of Repayment | Up to ten years; can consolidate |

---

### Nursing Student Loan (NSL)

| | |
|---|---|
| Annual Loan Limit | $4000 |
| Cumulative Loan Limit | $13,000 |
| Annual Interest Rate | 0% in school; 5% in repayment |
| Need-Based Aid | Yes |
| Application Fee | None |
| Creditworthiness Test | No |
| Origination Fee | None |
| Guarantee Fee | None |
| Form of Disbursement | Credited to student's account in two equal installments over the year |
| Deferments | No repayment while in school |
| Prepayment Penalty | No |
| Grace Period | Nine months |
| Minimum Monthly Payment | $15 |
| Length of Repayment | Up to ten years |

### Health Education Assistance Loan (HEAL)

| | |
|---|---|
| Annual Loan Limit | $20,000 |
| Cumulative Loan Limit | $80,000 |
| Variable Interest Rate | Variable, adjusted quarterly; Ninety-One-day T-Bill rate plus maximum 3.0% |
| Need-Based Aid | Yes |
| Application Fee | None |
| Creditworthiness Test | Yes |
| Origination Fee | Yes |
| Guarantee Fee | Yes (Note The origination and guarantee fees depend on the lender; the total combined is usually 8%) |
| Form of Disbursement | Check mailed directly to school |
| Deferments | Up to four years |
| Prepayment Penalty | No |
| Grace Period | Nine months |
| Minimum Monthly Payment | $50 |
| Length of Repayment | Up to twenty-five years |

### Primary Care Loan (PCL)

| | |
|---|---|
| Annual Loan Limit | Cost of tuition plus fees plus $2500 (depending on need) |
| Cumulative Loan Limit | None |
| Annual Interest Rate | 5% |
| Need-Based Aid | Yes |
| Application Fee | None |
| Creditworthiness Test | No |
| Origination Fee | None |
| Guarantee Fee | None |
| Form of Disbursement | Credited to student's account in two equal installments over the year |
| Deferments | No repayment while in school and during residency |
| Prepayment Penalty | None |
| Grace Period | 1 year |
| Minimum Monthly Payment | $15 |
| Length of Repayment | Up to 10 years |

## Entrance and Exit Interviews

As part of the effort to reduce default rates and curb costs, schools are required to conduct entrance and exit interviews with students who borrow under any of the federally guaranteed loan programs. During these sessions, the terms of the loan(s) are reviewed to make sure that you understand the commitment you are making. The school explains your borrower's rights and responsibilities, deferments, refinancing, loan-consolidation options, and your obligation to repay. After the exit interview, you should know exactly when the first payment is due and how much is expected.

## Default

It has become common practice for the media to publish stories about the extraordinary rate of student loan defaults. Although these stories are generally exaggerated, student loan defaults are, in fact, a serious problem—one that costs the federal government close to $2 billion annually.

For the Federal Stafford Loans, default occurs once you fail to make payments for 180 days (for loans repayable in monthly installments) or 240 days (for loans repayable in less frequent installments). For the Federal Perkins Loan, you are in default if you do not make payments for 120 days for monthly schedules or 180 days for less frequent payment schedules.

The consequences of default are serious. For one thing, you will be reported to national credit bureaus, which means that you may subsequently be prevented from obtaining credit of any kind, including credit cards, a home mortgage, or a car loan. Defaulters are also not permitted to obtain financial aid from other federal financial assistance programs. In more serious cases, defaulters can be taken to court, have their assets taken from them, have their wages garnished, and lose federal or state income tax refunds. Furthermore, defaulters may also be charged with legal fees for collecting the loan and may have difficulty obtaining employment in federal agencies.

For these reasons, it is wise to keep up-to-date on your loan repayments. If, for some reason, however, you cannot meet your monthly bills, you should contact your lender and make arrangements to pay *some* portion of your bill. It is up to your lender whether or not to grant extra time, but, in most cases, lenders will allow you to stop making payments temporarily or reduce the amount of your monthly payment until your financial situation improves. If this is the case, your lender will ask you to sign a Forbearance Agreement that indicates the length of extended time and the required payments under the new plan. It will be up to your lender to determine an adjusted payment schedule. Some may ask you to pay only the interest. Others may require that you add the accruing interest to the balance of your loan.

## Borrower's Rights and Responsibilities

Students who borrow from federal loan programs have the following rights and responsibilities:

### Rights

1. The promissory note you sign, agreeing to repay the loan with certain conditions, is a legally binding document. You must be given a copy of this agreement when you sign, and the original note must be returned to you when the loan is paid in full.
2. You have the right to a grace period before your repayment period begins if the loan terms provide for one. The grace period begins when you leave school or drop below half-time status. The exact length of your grace period is listed on your promissory note.
3. You must be given a list of deferment conditions and the conditions under which the Department of Education will repay your loan.
4. If you have a Federal Stafford Loan your loan proceeds must be made payable to you or to both you and your school.
5. Before your school gives you your first loan disbursement, your school or your lender must give you the following information about your loan:

    - the full amount of the loan, the interest rate, and when repayment begins

    - the effect borrowing will have on your eligibility for other types of financial aid

    - a complete list of any charges to the borrower, including loan fees, and information on how these charges are collected

    - the yearly and total amounts you can borrow and the maximum and minimum repayment periods

- a current description of the loans you owe your school or lender, an estimate of your total debt, and your monthly payments

- an explanation of default and its consequences; student loan defaults are reported to a credit bureau

- an explanation of refinancing and consolidation options and information on your option to prepay your loan at any time without penalty

6. Before your repayment period begins, your school or lender must provide you with the following information:

- the amount of your total debt, including principal and interest, what the interest rate is, and the total interest charges on your loan

- the name of your lender, where to send your payments, and where to write if you have questions about your loan

- what fees you should expect during the repayment period

- information about prepayment, refinancing, and consolidation options

- a loan repayment schedule that informs you when your first payment is due and the number, frequency, and amount of all payments

7. If you have a Federal Subsidized Stafford Loan, you have a right to receive federal interest benefits if you qualify. This means that the federal government pays the interest on your loan until your repayment period begins and also pays the interest on your loan during authorized deferment periods.

8. If you have a Federal Subsidized Stafford Loan and the lender sells the loan or transfers the right to receive payment, you must be notified.

## Responsibilities

1. You must notify your lender if you graduate, withdraw from school, or drop below half-time status.
2. You must notify your lender if you transfer to another school.
3. You must notify your lender if you change your name, address, or social security number.

4. You must notify your lender if you do not enroll in school for the period for which the loan is intended.

5. You must repay your loan according to the terms detailed on your repayment schedule.

6. You must make payments on your loan even if you do not receive a bill.

7. You must notify your lender or school if extenuating circumstances prevent you from meeting your loan obligations.

8. You must notify your lender and school of any extenuating circumstances affecting your deferment or cancellation status.

9. Before you leave school, you must attend an exit interview.

# FEDERAL WORK-STUDY PROGRAM

Federal Work-Study provides eligible students with employment opportunities, usually in public and private nonprofit organizations. Federal work-study funds pay up to 75 percent of your wages, with the remainder paid by the employing agency. The funds are available to graduate students who demonstrate financial need through the Federal Methodology. Not all schools have Federal Work-Study funds and some limit their funding to undergraduates.

To qualify for Federal Work-Study, you must be a U.S. citizen, national, or permanent resident; be enrolled in a degree or certificate program, in most instances at least half time (schools are allowed to use their work-study funds for students attending less than half time, but most do not); and be making satisfactory academic progress as determined by the graduate school.

Each school sets its own application deadline and work-study earnings limits. The dollar value of a work-study award depends on your financial need, the amount of money the school has to offer, and the aid you receive from other sources. Wages vary and are related to the type of work done. Occasionally, schools use work-study funds to pay teaching and research assistants. Work-study students may work part time during the academic year and full time in the summer.

If you receive Federal Work-Study as part of your financial aid package, you can often use this award creatively to initiate or help shape a job that best suits your needs. This must be done skillfully and with the help and approval of the Financial Aid Office. Consult this office to learn what job opportunities they currently have available, whether you are free to choose your own job, what the pay rates are, and what paperwork is required.

# STATE GOVERNMENT AID

Some states offer support for graduate study. In the past, those with the biggest programs have been California, Michigan, New York, Oklahoma, and Texas. Due to fiscal constraints, some states have had to reduce or entirely eliminate their financial aid programs for graduate study. Nevertheless, approximately $20 million each year is still awarded by the states for graduate study. Two-thirds of these awards are need based; one-third, merit-based. To qualify for a particular state's aid, a graduate student must be a resident of that state. In most states, residency is established after you have lived there for at least twelve consecutive months prior to enrolling in school.

You should contact your state scholarship office directly to determine what aid it offers. A list of state scholarship agencies can be found in Appendix G.

In addition, some states offer their own private loan programs. These programs may be subject to state funding cuts; however, if you are a resident of one of the following states, you may want to see what loan programs they have available.

**States with Private Loan Programs:**

Alaska Commission on
  Postsecondary Education
P.O. Box FP
Juneau, AK 99811
907-465-2962

Maine Educational Loan Authority
P.O. Box 549
Augusta, ME 04332
207-623-2600

Minnesota SELF Loan
Higher Education Coordination
  Board
400 Capitol Square Building
550 Cedar Street
St. Paul, MN 55101
612-296-3974

Pennsylvania HELP Program
660 Boas Street
Harrisburg, PA 17102
800-343-1809 (toll-free)

# 4 SERVICE-RELATED AWARDS AND LOANS

L ast fall, Ruth Wjockik graduated from New York University with an M.S. in library science. The degree qualified her for a promotion at the private library where she has been employed for the last six years. She *could* have gotten the promotion a long time ago, but she waited four years after graduating from college to enter a master's program. The reason was she didn't have the money.

"My parents are first-generation Poles," she says, "and, no matter how much I explained that it was okay to disclose their net financial worth, they steadfastly refused to do so. That left me ineligible for institutional aid. Because I have a full-time job, I also assumed I'd be ineligible for federal aid. One day, on a lark, I stopped in at the NYU aid office and, to my great surprise, found out that half of my graduate tuition could be covered through a variety of aid programs. I applied the very next day."

Ruth's experience is mirrored by many. Despite a widespread lack of knowledge about their existence, institutional aid programs channel between $3 billion and $4 billion to students each year. Funds are available through a variety of programs, among them, fellowships, tuition waivers, and assistantships. Let me again stress that some programs in the arts and sciences make awards on a merit basis, while the professional schools (law, business, medicine) generally fund their students more on the basis of need.

But there's more to private funding than institutional aid. Throughout the country, thousands of individuals, foundations, and corporate sponsors offer millions of dollars in financial support to graduate students who meet certain criteria. In this chapter you'll learn about some of these private sources of support: service-related awards and private loan programs. Later, in Chapter 5, we'll discuss private grant programs.

# INSTITUTIONAL WORK PROGRAMS AND SERVICE-RELATED AWARDS

After federal loans, the most common funding sources for graduate students are those that provide payment for performance of service. These can be classified into three general areas:

1. Assistantships, for which need may or may not be considered. They are normally awarded on the basis of an evaluation of academic performance.
2. Paid internships, which are usually taken for credit as part of a formal academic program. They are designed so that students can complete supervised practical training under the direction of experienced professionals.
3. Student employment that allows students to earn income through specially designed on-campus student-work programs or through regular employment in the private sector.

## Graduate Assistantships

Howard Adams, of the Graduate Education for Minorities Program, talks often about the importance of assistantships. "You've got to have a key to the lab," he has been known to say on numerous occasions. By that he means it is fine to get a fellowship for graduate study, but unless you are part of the professor's "group" (i.e., you are a research assistant) you don't have entry to the department in the same way you would had you been a research assistant. Don't be fooled into thinking it is always better to have "free money," that is, a fellowship. The contacts and experience you gain as a research assistant can sometimes be more valuable in the end than any amount of straight fellowship support. Adams's remarks are particularly true for doctoral students studying in science and engineering fields.

Much graduate support is given in the form of assistantships. In most cases you receive a stipend, that is, a paycheck which is sometimes paid in one lump sum each semester and sometimes paid over a period of weeks or months. Additionally, there is often either a partial or full tuition fee grant, or a partial or full tuition fee reduction. Again, practices vary widely from institution to institution. Some state institutions provide the equivalent of in-state or out-of-state tuition awards. Private institutions may separate the awarding of tuition grants entirely from the assistantship appointment. In most cases graduate assistantships require you to perform tasks related, but not necessarily contributing, to your academic work. Assistantships are most often awarded on the basis of merit and, therefore, can be quite competitive.

## Graduate Teaching Assistantships

Most schools with large undergraduate programs employ graduate teaching assistants (TA's). If you pursue an advanced degree in a subject that is taught at the undergraduate level—for example, in the arts and sciences—you may have a good chance of securing a teaching assistantship. Such a position may involve delivering lectures, correcting class work, grading papers, counseling students, and supervising laboratory groups. A standard teaching assistantship is a half-time appointment, i.e., a 20-hour-per-week commitment. Often such an assistantship will carry some fringe benefits with it, most often tuition remission or reduction and health insurance. Note that a teaching assistant's salary is now considered taxable income.

Teaching assistantships provide excellent educational experience as well as financial support. Appointments are based on academic qualifications and are subject to the availability of funds within an academic department. If you're interested in a teaching assistantship, you should contact the academic department in charge of such appointments. Ordinarily you will not be considered for such a position until after you've been admitted to graduate school. And, like other assistantships, these can be quite competitive, so be sure you convey your interest right away.

## Graduate Research Assistantships

As is the case with teaching assistantships, research assistantships provide excellent academic training as well as practical experience and financial support. Graduate research assistants receive financial support in return for assisting faculty with research projects. The bonus is that you are often able to work on research related to your own degree, especially if you are hired by one of your professors/mentors.

Research assistants (RA's) are most often funded by the grant money received by professors to carry out their own research. Research assistantships differ little from fellowships, except that you may be more constrained in your choice of dissertation topic and more dependent on your mentor. You may also risk losing your assistantship if your work is not compatible with that of your mentor, if it deviates from the overall research design, or if the research grant supporting the work is not renewed.

Some research assistants are funded by university endowments or by state money designed to facilitate faculty research. Other research assistants write their own research grants that are funded in their own right. As is the case with TA's, RA's are generally appointed to work some part of a 40-hour week. RA's who are working on their own dissertation topics, however, usually pay little attention to their presumed hours and often work long hours to get a project completed by a deadline.

Appointments are ordinarily made for one academic year. They are rarely offered to first-year students because the agencies providing the support are often reluctant to have their money given to inexperienced graduate students who have not yet proven themselves in graduate school. If you are interested in becoming an RA, you should contact the academic department in which you are enrolled and describe your particular research interests.

## Graduate Administrative Assistantships

At some schools assistantships exist that may not be under the jurisdiction of the graduate school. Sometimes called graduate administrative assistants or graduate associates, these students perform tasks in administrative and support services. Often the tasks are related to your particular field of interest, so that, for example, education majors become involved with audio-visual materials, computer scientists work with programming for the university, music students help with children's preparatory programs, physical education majors staff basketball camps, etc. These positions usually require 10 to 20 hours of work each week in an administrative office of the university.

Many graduate assistantships are not publicized or are publicized selectively, so finding them may be a matter of chance. As a result, some positions may go unfilled or go to less-qualified undergraduates in the absence of more experienced applicants.

As is the case with teaching and research assistants, graduate assistants are appointed to work some part of a 40-hour week, and many receive tuition support or a tuition waiver as well as a stipend or salary. Problems sometimes arise from the inclination to let the assistantship become a full-time job. Graduate assistants who do not work in the department in which they are enrolled are quite often viewed as employees who also happen to be students. Your supervisor may forget the demands placed on you as a student and encourage you to work too many hours.

Despite these hurdles, administrative assistantships can be a valuable source of support for graduate students. Details concerning these positions can be found in the school catalog or by directly contacting the academic department in which you would like to work.

## Residence Assistantships

Residence assistants help the residence director in undergraduate dormitories and in return for free room and board are often "on call" during the evenings and weekends to ensure that dormitory life runs smoothly.

It is common practice for residential universities to offer graduate students a variety of assistantship opportunities in their residence halls, including the position of residence director. In addition to a basic stipend, other financial assistance may be provided, such as free room and board.

---

## USE OF FEDERAL WORK-STUDY FUNDING

Although this is a federally funded program, it is important to mention it in this section of institutional support sources because Federal Work-Study can be an extremely valuable source of financial support for graduate students, and it is one that is often overlooked by both the graduate student and the institution.

Federal Work-Study is available to graduate students who demonstrate financial need and qualify for jobs in the non-profit sector, either on or off campus. Job selection, number of hours worked per week, and rate of pay vary from school to school, though it must be at least minimum wage. Often, the academic and personal needs of the students are generally considered. Schools that operate summer work-study programs usually offer the opportunity of work anywhere in the country. More details about Federal Work-Study are provided in Chapter 3. For further information, you should inquire at your individual school's Financial Aid Office.

---

## Internships

Internships outside the university are quickly becoming an integral part of many graduate programs, not just the professional schools. They provide practical experience conducted under the joint direction of an on-site supervisor and a campus-based mentor. Students may engage in independent investigations as part of the internship and provide written reports and evaluations of their experiences. It is common for interns to receive compensation directly from the cooperating entity; academic credit is normally granted by the university.

Internships have long been used by professional programs both to support graduate students financially and to give such students practical experience. More and more disciplines are seeking internship alliances with both public and private sector institutions outside the university as a way of enlarging their students' experiences, providing research materials, and obtaining financial support.

An additional benefit of internships is that, in some cases, they open avenues of permanent employment for graduates. Not all schools offer internships, and some do not offer academic credit for internship experience. Check with your school about its policy on internships.

## Cooperative Education

This program integrates work experience with academic study. At some schools you may earn academic credit for faculty-supervised employment in full-or part-time work assignments related to your educational and career interests and, at the same time, you are a salaried employee. You pay tuition for course credit in supervised, cooperative education field experience. Salaries vary, as does the administration of these programs from school to school. Schools that utilize cooperative education programs for their graduate students often have a placement office with a section devoted specifically to cooperative education.

There is a National Center for Cooperative Education located at Northeastern University, 360 Huntington Avenue, Boston, Massachusetts 02115. For more information on schools that offer graduate cooperative education, contact 617-373-3778.

## Additional Employment Opportunities

In addition to the types of positions described above, many schools provide on-campus employment opportunities that do not require you to demonstrate financial need. The Student Employment Office on most campuses assists students in securing jobs both on and off the campus.

## Employment Referral Services

Even for full-time students, employment at off-campus locations provides a means of generating additional income. At many institutions student employment and/or financial aid offices provide an information service for off-campus employment opportunities.

At Georgetown University, for example, the Employment Referral Service (ERS) helps Georgetown students find part-time and temporary jobs in the Washington, D.C., metropolitan area by acting as a clearinghouse for job listings from local businesses, individuals, and organizations. The service lists various opportunities, from temporary jobs to skilled office positions, that last throughout the entire school year. Any currently enrolled Georgetown University student may register with the ERS. The program can be particularly helpful to students who are not eligible for the Federal Work-Study Program but who need to work to help meet expenses.

# PRIVATE AND INSTITUTIONAL LOAN PROGRAMS

A number of colleges and universities—especially those that offer professional degree programs that generally cost more than research degrees—have their own loan programs or participate in privately funded loan programs. The following are examples of such loan programs at law, medical, and business schools; the examples are followed by samples of some general graduate loan programs. The terms and conditions of these loans change frequently so it is advisable to contact the lender directly for the current borrowing information.

## Law School

If you are thinking about applying to law school, you should be prepared to borrow. Much of the financial aid available for those interested in studying law is in the form of loans. This section will discuss the various private sources of funding for law students.

Georgetown University, like some other law schools, offers a unique "grant" program for its law students. Those who receive this Georgetown "grant," often given through the generosity of alumni, foundations, and other friends of the university, are awarded these funds with the understanding that they have a moral obligation to repay the funds received by contributing to the law school after they graduate. While there are no legal obligations to pay back the money, graduates are reminded that without this support, they would have been unable to attend.

Other law schools have their own institutional loan funds. The schools set the interest rates and repayment terms.

## Law Access Loan

The Access Group offers a comprehensive program through which law students can borrow Federal Stafford Loans as well as private loans for law school and for the bar examination study period. With the Law Access Loan (LAL), creditworthy law students may borrow from a minimum amount of $500 to a maximum total outstanding debt of $120,000 (which includes undergraduate and graduate study).

For the in-school and interim periods, the interest rate varies quarterly based on the 91-day Treasury Bill rate plus 3.25 percent. At repayment, the interest rate varies quarterly based on the 91-day Treasury Bill rate plus 3.4 percent. Interest is capitalized once, when repayment begins. There is a guarantee fee of 8 percent that is subtracted at disbursement. An additional 2 percent is added to the principal of the loan immediately prior to repayment. There is no origination fee. Repayment begins nine months after graduation, or when a borrower's status drops to less than half-time. Borrowers have up to twenty years to repay.

The Access Group's bar examination loan, called the Bar Examination Loan (BEL), assists graduating students with the expenses they incur while studying for the bar exam. Students in their last semester of law school can borrow up to $5,000 from the Bar Exam Loan program. Credit requirements and loan terms are very similar to the Law Access Loan.

For more information on Law Access Loans or Bar Examination Loans, contact the financial aid office of your law school or call The Access Group at 800-282-1550.

## LawLoans

Like Law Access Loans, LawLoans offers a comprehensive student loan program through which law students can borrow Federal Stafford Loans, a Law Student Loan (LSL), and a Bar Study Loan. Although the Bar Study Loan requires a separate application, only one application is needed to apply for the other loans. After graduating from law school, borrowers can arrange through Sallie Mae, loan consolidation called, the SMART LOAN Account for lawyers.

To be eligible for the Law Student Loans a student must be enrolled in an approved American Bar Association (ABA) law school (not all law schools are eligible for the LSL program), be a citizen or national of the U.S., or be a permanent resident with proper evidence of eligibility. All outstanding student loans must be in good standing, i.e. not in default. The maximum amount borrowed cannot exceed the cost of attendance less other financial aid for which the student is eligible. Creditworthy law students can borrow $15,000 per year up to a maximum of $60,000, and $100,000 with a cosigner. The total unpaid educational loans from all sources must be $102,500 or less, or $150,000 with a cosigner. A first time borrower must borrow a minimum of $1,000 and continuing borrowers must borrow a minimum of $500.

The interest rate varies quarterly. The rate is based on the bond equivalent average of the 91-day Treasury Bill plus 3.25 percent. At repayment there is a choice of variable rates adjusted quarterly, which will not exceed the 91-day Treasury Bill plus 3.5 percent or will not exceed the 10-year U.S. Treasury Bonds plus 4.5 percent. There is also a guarantee fee of 7.5 percent for cosigned loans. For loans that are not cosigned, the guarantee fee is 7.5 percent at disbursement plus an additional fee added at repayment. (Currently, this fee is 3.25 percent but may be adjusted at the insurer's discretion.)

Repayment begins nine months after graduation or when your student status drops to less than half time prior to graduation. You have fifteen years to repay.

Students applying for a Bar Study Loan (BSL) from LawLoans must be in their final year in an ABA-approved law school and have indicated an approximate date that they will take the bar exam, which is within six months of graduation from law school. In addition, the student must have previously secured either a Federal Stafford loan or LSL from LawLoans and apply and qualify for a minimum of a $500 loan. Creditworthy law students can apply for a loan up to $7,500.

The interest rate varies quarterly. The rate is the same as the LSL. The guarantee fee for cosigned loans is 6.5 percent and is 11 percent for loans that are not cosigned.

Repayment begins nine months after graduation or when your status drops to less than half time prior to graduation.

For more information on either the BSL or the LSL program call LawLoans Customer Service 800-366-5626.

## LawSHARE

The New England Loan Marketing Association (Nellie Mae) offers a loan program for law students called LawSHARE. Students can borrow up to $15,000 without a cosigner or up to the cost of attendance with a cosigner, with a cumulative maximum debt of $80,000. Eligibility for LawSHARE is based on creditworthiness, not financial need. A parent, sibling, spouse, or other responsible person can be the primary borrower. Students can choose either a variable interest rate (prime rate for the first year, and prime rate plus .5 percent after the first year), or a fixed interest rate (prime rate plus 2 to 3 percent). There is a guarantee fee of 6 percent with a cosigner and 9 percent without a cosigner, as well as a 2 percent capitalization fee. For more information contact Nellie Mae, 50 Braintree Hill Park, Suite 300, Braintree, MA 02184, 800-634-9308.

## Loan Forgiveness Programs

To try to offset the high levels of indebtedness law students face, some law schools have developed programs that offer "forgiveness" provisions for those students who enter low-paying legal positions in the area of public service. Georgetown University, for example, has such a program whereby the Georgetown Law Center lends funds to graduate students working in public interest law who have annual student loan payments from law school that exceed a certain percentage of their income. The Loan Repayment Assistance Program (LRAP) applies only to need-based loans (i.e., Federal Stafford/GSL, Federal Perkins/NDSL, Federal SLS/ALS, and Georgetown Law Center loans). Undergraduate and commercial loans, such as Law Access Loans, Law Student Loans, or LawSHARE loans, are not included.

At Georgetown there are three major requirements for participation in the LRAP. First, the law graduate must be employed or self-employed full time in a law-related capacity by an organization that, as one of its primary purposes, provides legal services to or on the behalf of people or organizations that could not otherwise obtain similar services. (Examples of eligible organizations include public defender's offices, the Washington Legal Foundation, and the American Civil Liberties Union. Examples of ineligible employment include clerkships, military service, government employment, and district attorney offices.)

Second, the graduate must enter qualifying employment within two years of graduation from Georgetown. For eligibility a graduate is expected to contribute one-half of all yearly income in excess of $28,325 toward his or her student loan debt. (Note: the proportion and salary limits differ for graduates who are married or who have dependents.)

Third, a graduate must arrange for consolidation of all federally sponsored loans under a 15- to 25-year repayment program.

There are also some state-based loan forgiveness opportunities. The National Association of Public Interest Law (NAPIL), based in Washington, D.C., maintains information on states that offer loan forgiveness programs. You can call NAPIL at 202-466-3686. For additional information on loan forgiveness programs, you should contact the Financial Aid Office at your school.

## Medical School

According to a recent survey, the median net income of all physicians was about $176,000. While most people's income falls far below that amount, physicians' high salaries are in part offset by the amount of debt they incur while at medical school. For students whose means are limited, acquiring debts in excess of $100,000 is very common. The average indebtedness at Georgetown (for those who did not receive military scholarships), for example, is over $100,000 (for those who did not receive military scholarships).

Debt repayment at this level is comparable to a home mortgage and must be taken very seriously. Borrowing means obligating future income. As the Office of Student Financial Planning at Georgetown stresses in it's annual publication to medical students, "Every dollar borrowed can cost as much as $3 to $7 (or more) in repayment, depending on the interest rate, the length of repayment, and the mode of repayment (e.g., equal monthly payments, graduated payments, etc.)."

In the past few years, several private loan programs for medical students have been created. Chief among these are the Medical Access Loan and AAMC MedLoans, through which medical students can apply for Federal Stafford and private loans.

## AAMC MedLoans

The Association of American Medical Colleges (AAMC) offers the Alternative Loan Program (ALP) for medical students.

Under the ALP program, you can borrow up to $30,000 a year, provided you are a U.S. citizen, enrolled full time, making satisfactory academic progress, creditworthy, and not in default on any student loans. The amount you borrow from all sources, including ALP, cannot exceed $30,000 for one year, and your total aggregate debt cannot exceed $120,000.

An insurance fee of 6 percent is deducted from the proceeds of the loan if you agree to pay the interest throughout the life of the loan, including the in-school period. If the lender determines that you are unable to pay the interest while you are in school, you may still obtain an ALP loan, but the insurance fee will be 8 percent. The interest rate is variable and is determined on a quarterly basis by adding 2.7 percent to the 91-day Treasury Bill.

With this type of loan you can obtain deferments of up to three to four years for postgraduate training, depending on the length of your residency. Once repayment of both principal and interest begins, you have ten years to repay the ALP loan. There is no penalty for prepayment. For more information on MedLoans, contact your school's Financial Aid Office.

For more information on medical school financial aid, consult the Association of American Medical Colleges, 2450 N Street, NW, Washington, D.C., 20037.

## Medical Access Loans

The Medical Access Loan program, sponsored by The Access Group, is dedicated exclusively to providing loan funds for medical studies. The Medical Access program allows for an outstanding educational debt of $165,000 (which includes undergraduate and graduate debt). For the in-school and interim periods, the interest rate varies quarterly based on the 91-day Treasury Bill rate plus 2.75 percent. Interest is capitalized at graduation and again at repayment. The guarantee fee is 6.5 percent at disbursement. An additional 2 percent is added to the principal of the loan immediately prior to repayment. There is no origination fee. Repayment begins nine months after graduation, or after the borrower's status drops to less than half-time, or after completion of a required medical residency program (not to exceed forty-eight months). Borrowers have up to twenty years to repay.

For more information, contact your medical school or The Access Group at 800-282-1550.

## MedSHARE

The New England Loan Marketing Association (Nellie Mae) offers a loan program for medical and dental students called MedSHARE. Students can borrow up to $20,000 without a cosigner or up to the cost of attendance with a cosigner, with a cumulative debt of $120,000 for medical students and $90,000 for dental students. In the final year of medical/dental school, students may borrow up to an additional $5,000. Eligibility for MedSHARE is based on creditworthiness, not financial need. A parent, sibling, spouse, or other responsible person can be the primary borrower. Students can choose either a variable interest rate (prime rate for the first year, and prime rate plus .5 percent after the first year), or a fixed interest rate (prime rate plus 2 to 3 percent). There is a guarantee fee as well as a capitalization fee. For more information contact Nellie Mae, 50 Braintree Hill Park, Suite 300, Braintree, MA 02184, 800-634-9308.

## Business School

Like law and medicine, specific loans for students attending business schools are available. Details on such business programs follow.

## Business Access Loan Program

Sponsored by The Access Group, this program allows students attending business school a maximum total outstanding educational debt of $120,000 (which includes undergraduate and graduate debt). The maximum annual loan amount for less than half-time students is limited to the cost of tuition, fees, and up to $500 for books and supplies. For the in-school and interim periods, the interest rate varies quarterly based on the 91-day Treasury Bill rate plus 3.25 percent. At repayment, the interest rate varies quarterly based on the 91-day Treasury Bill rate plus 3.4 percent. Interest is capitalized once at repayment. The guarantee fee is 6.5 percent at disbursement. An additional 2 percent is added to the principal of the loan immediately prior to repayment. There is no origination fee. Repayment begins nine months after graduation, or after the borrower ceases to be enrolled, or three years after the first disbursement, whichever comes first. Borrowers have up to twenty years to repay.

For more information, contact your business school or The Access Group at 800-282-1550.

## MBA Loans and the Tuition Loan Plan (TLP)

This program is also designed to meet the financing needs of students enrolled in a graduate-level business school at least half-time. Applicants must be U.S. citizens or have lived in the United States for a minimum of three years.

The annual TLP loan maximum is $13,500 with a limit of $25,000. Total unpaid educational loans from all sources cannot exceed $60,000. The maximum amount you may borrow is based on your estimated educational expenses minus other financial aid. The TLP interest rate is either variable or fixed; the variable rate is adjusted quarterly and is based on the average 91-day Treasury Bill plus 3.5 percent. The fixed rate is based on the Treasury Bill rate plus 4.5 percent. Interest accrues while you are in school but may be deferred until six months after you leave school. Deferred interest is capitalized and added to principal once, at repayment.

There's a guarantee fee of 7.5 percent for loans that are cosigned; for loans that are not cosigned, there is a 7.5 percent guarantee fee at disbursement plus an additional amount (currently 3.25 percent) added at repayment. There are no origination or application fees. Repayment of MBA loans begins six months after you graduate or drop to less than half-time status. You have a maximum of twelve years to repay the loan. For more information on MBA loans, contact your school's Financial Aid Office.

## MBASHARE

The New England Loan Marketing Association (Nellie Mae) offers a loan program for M.B.A. students called MBASHARE. Students can borrow up to $15,000 without a cosigner or up to the cost of attendance with a cosigner, with a cumulative debt of $80,000. Eligibility for MBASHARE is based on creditworthiness, not financial need. A parent, sibling, spouse, or other responsible person can be the primary borrower. Students can choose either a variable interest rate (prime rate for the first year, and prime rate plus .5 percent after the first year), or a fixed interest rate (prime rate plus 2 to 3 percent). There is a guarantee fee of 5 percent with a cosigner and 8 percent without a cosigner, as well as a 2 percent capitalization fee. For more information contact: Nellie Mae, 50 Braintree Hill Park, Suite 300, Braintree, MA 02184, 800-634-9308.

# OTHER PRIVATE SOURCES FOR ALTERNATIVE LOANS

The loan programs described below are not tied to any one profession and are worth considering if you are not going to law, medical, or business school. Some are based on need; others are based solely on creditworthiness.

## AchieverLoan

The Knight College Resource Group provides an AchieverLoan, a personal, unsecured loan designed exclusively for education purposes. The AchieverLoan has three flexible financing options: the Multiple Year Option, the Annual Option, and the Interest-Only option. The interest rate for the Multiple Year Option is set to the 13-week Treasury Bill rate plus 3.95 percent. The Annual Option and Interest-Only option have an interest rate set quarterly to the 13-week Treasury Bill plus 4.5 percent. For more information contact the Knight College Resource Group at 800-225-6783 ext. 345 to speak with a representative about the options available to you.

## The Education Resources Institute (TERI)

The Education Resources Institute sponsors a loan program for students and their families. It is available for study at any accredited institution of higher education in any state. To qualify, applicants must demonstrate creditworthiness, and either the borrower or the cosigner must be a U.S. citizen. There is no needs test or upper income limit. Amounts, interest rates, and repayment plans vary.

TERI loans include the TERI Alternative Loan, which is available to students and their parents to provide financing up to the cost of education less financial aid; the Professional Education Plan (PEP), available to graduate and professional students; and several specialized graduate programs for students in chiropractic, osteopathic, optometric, veterinary, physical therapy, physician's assistant, nursing, or occupational therapy fields. For more information contact: TERI at 800-255-TERI.

## Graduate Access Loans

The Graduate Access Loan program, sponsored by The Access Group, allows those students attending graduate school a maximum total outstanding educational debt of $120,000 (including both undergraduate and graduate debt). For the in-school and interim period, the interest rate varies quarterly based on the 91-day Treasury Bill rate plus 3.25 percent. At repayment, the interest rate varies quarterly based on the 91-day Treasury Bill rate plus 3.40 percent. Interest is capitalized once at repayment. The guarantee fee is 7.0 percent at disbursement. An additional 2.0 percent is added to the principal of the loan immediately prior to repayment. There is no origination fee. Repayment begins nine months after graduation, or if the student's status drops to less than half-time. Borrowers have up to twenty years to repay. For more information, contact your graduate school or The Access Group at 800-282-1550.

## GradSHARE

The New England Loan Marketing Association (Nellie Mae) offers a loan program for graduate students called GradSHARE. Students can borrow up to $12,000 without a cosigner or up to the cost of attendance with a cosigner, with a cumulative debt of $50,000, or $65,000 for engineering students. Eligibility for GradSHARE is based on creditworthiness, not financial need. A parent, sibling, spouse, or other responsible person can be the primary borrower. Students can choose either a variable interest rate (prime rate for the first year, and prime rate plus .5 percent after the first year), or a fixed interest rate (prime rate plus 2 to 3 percent). There is a guarantee fee of 6 percent with a cosigner and 9 percent without a cosigner, as well as a 2 percent capitalization fee. For more information contact: Nellie Mae, 50 Braintree Hill Park, Suite 300, Braintree, MA 02184, 800-634-9308.

## Option 4 Loan Program

This loan program through USA Funds is a private, alternative education loan designed to help students and their families pay college costs. Under the Option 4 Loan Program, you can borrow up to $15,000 per year per student and take up to fifteen years to repay on manageable repayment terms. The interest rate on an Option 4 Loan is a variable rate equal to the average quarterly bond equivalent rate of 91-day Treasury Bills plus 3.5 percent. Students and parents of students enrolled or accepted for enrollement at least half-time at an approved college or university are eligible to apply for an Option 4 Loan. Applicant approval is based on creditworthiness and current ability to repay the loan. There is no needs test. At least one borrower must be a U.S. citizen. For more information contact: USA Funds, P.O. Box 6198, Indianapolis, IN 46206-6198, 800-635-3785.

## Home Equity Loans and Lines of Credit

For those who have equity in a home, many commercial lenders are offering home equity loans, some at very attractive rates with extended repayment periods. Furthermore, if the proceeds go toward educational costs, the interest on the loan is tax deductible. Often the bank with which you have your first mortgage will offer you an attractive rate on a home equity loan as a good customer. But you should also shop around for the best deal (e.g., no application fees, drive-by appraisals, low rates, etc.).

## Tuition Payment Plans

Many universities and graduate schools provide monthly tuition payment plans that allow you to pay all or part of your tuition costs in monthly installments, some without interest charges. These plans can be used to supplement other forms of financial aid, or they can be used by those who do not receive any financial aid. Consult your intended school's Student Accounts or Bursar's Office to determine if they have such a plan.

## Short-Term Loans

Some schools operate a short-term loan program for their enrolled students. These loans are usually only given to assist in unanticipated situations. Nominal interest rates may or may not be charged. Consult your Financial Aid Office for information about such loans.

# FINDING AND APPLYING FOR GRANTS

Most students approach the search for graduate school research grants with fear and trepidation. Some are ashamed that they have to apply for money; others are worried that no one will want to fund them. Still others are overwhelmed at the thought of preparing a proposal. Experience has shown that the most productive attitude for a student to take when beginning the grant-seeking process is to treat it as (1) a learning experience—part of graduate education as a whole (in fact, the skills and strategies used to find grant sources and apply for grant money are similar to those needed to find many postgraduate jobs) and (2) a partnership between the recipient and the sponsor.

## Grant Seeking as a Learning Experience

"When I first started searching for a grant to support my master's program in geography, I had only the vaguest idea what I wanted to do with the degree once I got it," says Moira Shannon, an environmental specialist with Wells Fargo Bank. "It was only in looking through the kinds of available funding that I discovered the need for people to work in Third World countries guiding corporations toward environmentally safe practices. The particular grant I applied for—and got—was to study the economic aftereffects of clearing vast areas of the rain forest. It became the focus of my program as well as the nature of my postgraduate employment specialty."

The grant-seeking process often helps you think logically and focus your ideas as you plan your whole graduate program. Preparing a proposal requires thinking through ideas and conclusions carefully, and, as in Moira Shannon's case, the process can also help shape career plans after graduate school.

A search for grant support might also help in narrowing a specific aspect of a research topic for a dissertation. If a number of grant possibilities are found to support research in a particular area, you might choose to concentrate on that area. One aspect of doing research, after all, is the ability to carry it out, which is often directly related to the ability to get it funded.

Also, the process of searching for grants while you're still a student will make you familiar with many of the sponsoring organizations and with the entire process of seeking financial support. You'll gain confidence that will help you maneuver through the world of grants. Later in your career you'll likely need to prepare full-blown proposals for money, whether to obtain venture capital for a fledgling business or to get grant money for a corporate research project. The experience you gain seeking grants for graduate school will make the tasks seem less bewildering and overwhelming.

## A Partnership Between Recipients and Sponsors

In order for research and related projects to be carried out, funds must be available to support them. It is the rare person, however, who has both the ideas and skills to conduct a research project *and* the direct access to the funds necessary to do so. The researcher and the sponsor, then, are equally important elements in the funding equation. Each needs the other. Researchers, or students who have ideas and projects in mind, contribute to the creativity and expertise; sponsors with funds at their command contribute financial support. When these two ingredients come together in a partnership, a successful project can result.

But what does the sponsor expect to get back from the recipient in exchange for financial support? In some cases, you merely have to write a quarterly progress report; in others, you'll need to submit a thickly bound summary resembling a thesis. Some organizations ask you to provide service. The Council on Secondary Education, for example, requires you to work for two years in ghetto areas in exchange for full funding of your graduate program.

Commitment and accountability are of utmost importance to a funding organization. If you say you'll undertake a certain project, the sponsor expects you to follow through to the project's completion. In some cases, funding is provided with the specific stipulation that you not engage in certain activities, such as publicly promoting products in competition with those of the funding organization; it is expected that you will, indeed, adhere to any stipulations. Many corporations refuse to fund individuals, preferring to give their money to institutions that are more accountable for the actions of their researchers. For this reason—to respect the trust placed in you as an individual—it is imperative that you honor the agreement made with a sponsoring organization. Never commit to projects you have no intention of completing.

Academic honesty is also expected of all individuals accepting grant money. Never submit another person's work and never falsify your results. Sponsors take honesty seriously and often try to prevent deception by requiring that advisers and graduate deans recommend both the student and the proposed research project.

In almost all cases, you are asked to adhere to the goals of the sponsoring organization. This, for better or for worse, is part of the partnership equation. These goals are usually spelled out in the grant program description announcement. If you feel in conflict with the organization's goals, it is best not to apply for that particular grant in the first place. Remember that, as a funding recipient, you will be seen as reflecting the ideology of your sponsor. With this in mind, you should concentrate your efforts on sponsors with whom you feel ideologically comfortable.

## Where Is The Money?

Unfair though it may be, the funds available to support graduate students are not evenly distributed among disciplines. Some fields, like the sciences, have more programs and more money than others. For instance, research efforts in the sciences are generally well-funded. This will become more than obvious as you glance through the samples of grant listings arranged by discipline later in this chapter.

An increasing amount of money is available for study or research related to women's studies and Third World studies (e.g., The Woodrow Wilson National Fellowship Foundation's Women's Studies Research Grants or the dissertation awards of Radcliffe's Henry A. Murray Research Center). There are also many organizations that support minority graduate students and others that support women in graduate school. For example, the Business and Professional Women's Foundation is set up to help mature women embark on graduate studies. International students studying in the United States will find a few programs designed to meet their study and research needs. Chapter 6 contains information on aid for specific student groups—international students studying in the United States, Americans studying abroad, minorities, women, and veterans.

Funding also exists to support research drawn on the collections of a number of libraries across the country, with the libraries providing the funds themselves and requiring residencies at the collection.

In addition, fellowships to support students while they are primarily taking courses—in other words, for students who are not, at the moment, available to do research, are difficult to obtain. Travel awards are also rare, especially those covering travel to a meeting or conference, large sums (enough money to support a family, even the most generous awards provide only $10,000 to $14,000 for living expenses), and money to cover expenses incurred prior to the starting date of the award.

As a general rule, it is more difficult to find awards in the humanities, business and management, and education.

## Success Through Trading Up

"When I first started looking for grant money, I was naturally drawn to the big awards," says Lee Fong, who is in the final year of a doctoral program in chemical engineering. "Instead, I obtained a few in the $500 to $1,000 range. Now that I'm almost finished with my dissertation, however, I'm being told I'm a prime candidate for larger awards in the $7,500 to $12,000 range."

Not all students are immediately ready or able to compete for large awards. Don't let that discourage you. As you begin your quest, you'll find that there are many smaller grants that are an ideal springboard to "trading up" for larger awards later, especially for the new graduate student. There are two reasons why trading up can help you. First, sponsors look with favor on individuals who have already won previous awards, regardless of the amounts. What that tells them is that you've been through the review process and have come out a winner. You know how to locate funding sources, know how to present yourself, and know how to plead your case successfully. These are all attractive attributes in terms of future—and possibly larger—awards.

Second, the application process for smaller awards often is not nearly as painful or time-consuming as that for larger ones. Chances are that for a $350 award, a page or two will be required, as opposed to the twenty-plus pages required for a $10,000 award. And should you be successful in getting a small award, you'll have mastered at least some of the steps to successful grant-writing—an ability that will serve you well when you apply for larger sums of money.

# FIVE STEPS TO GETTING GRANTS

## Step 1: Define Your Project

The first step in locating appropriate programs is to get your thoughts in order. While it may seem that the process entails only finding the source and mailing the application, the reality is that finding grant sources depends on your being very clear about both your reasons for wanting money as well as who you are as a candidate. Answering the following questions should get you on the right track:

- For what type of project are you seeking funds? Will it be a survey? a statistical comparison? a service experience? an investigative exposé?

- What is the subject area for which you are requesting funds? Women's studies, for example, may be too broad—you'll need to narrow it down to, say, women's literature or women's health.

- What constituency will be affected by your project? Will it, for example, benefit minorities? Third World inhabitants?

- Where will you do your project? Does it involve travel, living in a dangerous area? Is your chosen location the best place to carry out this project?

- How long will your project take? Will you need flexibility? In other words, if you're not finished by the stated time, will you need more money?

- What is the purpose of this project? How will it benefit you, your target population, and—most of all—your sponsor?

- How much money will you need?

## Step 2: Determine What Kind of Money You Need

After you define the project needs, you have to determine whether the money you need includes living expenses or just the expenses related to the project. Your level of study might determine this choice for you. During the first few years of study, for example, you'll be taking courses rather than working on your own projects, so your needs will be more along the line of living expenses. Later on, during the final phase of master's or doctoral study, you may need grant support to finance your research projects. You might, however, be looking for neither, but rather for travel funds—possibly for a summer internship that involves living in another geographic location.

## Step 3: Define Your Field of Interest

The next step is to define as completely as possible your field of interest. Make a list of both general and specific key words that apply to your topic to help you define your interests. Such a list will help when it comes to looking through directories (either printed or computerized) that are organized according to topic. Don't forget the geographical location of the study and the nature of your constituency. For example, a project studying the relationship between freedom of dress and women's economic progress in present-day Saudi Arabia might be identified by the following key words:

- women's studies
- geography
- Saudi Arabia
- economics
- fashion
- comparative religions
- sexism
- division of labor
- Arab customs
- Islam
- Third World countries
- wearing the veil
- behavioral-social sciences
- cross-cultural studies
- feminism
- law
- politics
- cultural differences
- tradition

Or, to use an example from the natural sciences, a research project to study the maintenance of habitats for the spotted owl in the forests of the Pacific Northwest might employ the following key words:

- science
- environment
- reproductive biology
- old forest growth
- Washington
- Oregon
- timber industry
- owls
- wildlife
- conservation
- natural resources
- economics
- species extinction

## Step 4: Define Your Financial Needs

The fourth step is to define the project in terms of its duration and financial needs. The following are samples of such definitions:

- a three-month project to take place at the Musee d'Orsay for which $3,000 to support living expenses is needed

- a summer research project in Africa with combined living, travel, and research expenses totaling $12,000

- $200 to $300 to cover postage and the printing of a questionnaire

- a two-year fellowship, preferably one that pays $6,000 to $8,000 per year

Make sure you ask for all that you need. It's of little use to apply for $500 when what you really need is $4,000. Sponsors want to feel that their money will be used productively. While they may not be familiar with *your* particular area of research, they are aware of costs, and one of the criteria used in approving or rejecting an award may be how realistic they sense you to be in assessing costs.

## Step 5: Defining Yourself

Finally, once you have defined the nature of your study and the funds needed to carry out the project and/or living expenses, you'll need to explain why you should get the grant. Personal characteristics can be quite important when searching for funds—especially when eligibility requirements are specifically related to the person who established the award. Some grants, for example, seek evidence of your patriotic fervor; some, your ideological alignment with the goals of the company; some, your ability to create a sizable amount of public relations.

With this in mind, questions like age, marital status, ethnic group, veteran status, grade point average, organizational affiliations, religion, and sorority or fraternity membership can all become important criteria for acceptance or rejection. Such criteria, however, come into play more in the awarding of fellowships that are geared toward professional development and that concentrate more on the individual as a person.

Ask yourself what personal qualities you will be seeking to project and how you will prove yourself to have those qualities. Many grant applications specify, for example, that you must have leadership qualities or be a person of good character. How will you demonstrate that you are a leader?

# A MARKETING APPROACH TO GETTING FUNDING

"I spent an entire year trying to get a grant to support my doctoral research," says Elaine Schwartz, a research scientist studying chemical dependencies. "No matter how many applications I sent out, I always got back a polite rejection. Finally, at a party, I met a woman who was in charge of corporate grants for Revlon. I told her my saga and asked what I was doing wrong. Know what she said? That I was looking at the whole thing too much from my perspective. 'What's in it for your sponsor?' she asked. In one minute's time she changed my whole approach."

The number one mistake students make seeking funding is assuming that the process is about finding a grant to meet *their* needs. The truth is exactly the reverse. Here's why: Imagine yourself in charge of handing out large sums of money to support student research. Even if you're very philanthropically oriented and seek no remuneration from the research, you're still subject to the wide variety of possibilities for your money and you will likely establish some criteria for distributing it. What would be your criteria—even if you were the most broad-minded of individuals? Obviously, you would seek to award money to those who, in some way, were like you, had the same goals as you, or were interested in the same things.

And therein lies your grant-seeking strategy. What you should be doing instead of spending all your time thinking about your own needs is to put yourself in the minds of the funding sources and try to figure out *their* needs.

All programs—whether federal or private—are organized with a specific goal in mind, often to advance a particular area of research or scholarship. Your goal, as a potential grant recipient, is to demonstrate your understanding of those goals and to prove your desire to advance them. Grant seekers, therefore, should first gather as much information as possible about the funding source and then use this information to develop a proposal rather than take an already-developed proposal and shape it to fit the goals of the funding source.

## MATCHING YOUR PROJECT TO FUNDING OPPORTUNITIES

The key to finding a grant is to identify the sponsor's goals or needs and then, through your work, to help fulfill them. A corollary to this approach is to survey the grants market before you decide on a research project, thesis, or dissertation project. Once you have determined where the funding opportunities lie, you can develop your project to best match those opportunities and thereby increase your chances of getting aid. While some feel this approach is too market-driven ("But what about the integrity of my research?"), the fact remains that you are asking someone to pay for your studies and should therefore be prepared to make at least some compromises in return.

# SOURCES OF FUNDING INFORMATION

You can obtain funding information by reading program announcements, reading annual reports, or calling or writing the sponsor directly. The *Federal Register* lists federal programs offering grant support and can be found in most libraries; it contains a wealth of information. For private sources, the following books provide considerable information on individual foundations and corporations:

*Annual Register of Grant Support: A Directory of Funding Sources.* Wilmette, Ill.: National Register Publishing.
    A comprehensive guide to grants and awards from government agencies, foundations, and business and professional organizations.

*Corporate Foundation Profiles.* 8th ed. New York: The Foundation Center, 1994.
    An in-depth, analytical profile of 250 of the largest company-sponsored foundations in the United States. Brief descriptions of the 700 company-sponsored foundations are also included. There is an index of subjects, types of support, and geographical locations.

*The Foundation Directory.* 20th ed. Edited by Stan Olson. New York: The Foundation Center, 1994.
    This directory, with supplement, gives detailed information on U.S. Foundations, with brief descriptions of their purposes and activities.

*The Grants Register 1995-97.* 14th ed. Edited by Lisa Williams. New York: St. Martin's Press, 1995.

Lists grant agencies alphabetically and gives information on awards available to graduate students, young professionals, and scholars for study and research.

*Peterson's Guide to Scholarships, Grants, and Prizes.* Princeton, NJ: Peterson's, 1996.
Profiles nearly 2,000 programs offering money for undergraduate and graduate students in every major field of study. Accompanying software allows users to search categories and print out a list of selected programs.

*Scholarships, Fellowships, and Loans 1994-95: A Guide to Education-Related Financial Aid Programs for Students and Professionals.* 10th ed. Edited by Debra M. Kirby. Gale Research, Inc., 1994.
Lists U.S. foundations and agencies offering financial support for undergraduate research and study. Sources are primarily for U.S. citizens or U.S. permanent residents, although some of the information may be helpful to international students.

Graduate schools sometimes publish listings of support sources in their catalogs, and some provide separate publications. One such example is the *Graduate Guide to Grants*, compiled by the Harvard Graduate School of Arts and Sciences (GSAS). You can get a copy by sending $23 (includes shipping and handling) to GSAS, 8 Garden Street, Cambridge, MA 02138 or by calling 617-495-1814.

Other excellent sources are the numerous databases that contain computerized information on the various grants, fellowships, independent project resources, and other available funding. Contact your school to see if it has access to any of these databases:

*The Stanford University Scholarships and Fellowships File.* This database was designed specifically for graduate students by Stanford University (with the assistance of the University of California at Berkeley, and Yale University). It has been expanded to include undergraduate sources as well. The Stanford database provides information about graduate entry-level fellowships, dissertation fellowships, postdoctoral fellowships, research opportunities, funding for independent projects, and some loans.

This on-line mainframe database contains more than 1,700 graduate entries (and 1,600 undergraduate entries) and is updated regularly. About a dozen schools have purchased the database, which can be used for a fee of $15 per hour. Instructions appear on the screen to guide the user through the steps necessary to access the appropriate information. The database can be accessed through the World Wide Web on the Internet at no cost to the university.

*IRIS—Illinois Researcher Information System.* Developed by the University of Illinois at Urbana-Champaign, this on-line information retrieval system is designed to identify and provide current information on more than 6,000 sources supporting research and scholarship activities available to faculty, staff, and students. This database is updated daily and is available by subscription through Internet and several other telecommunications sources.

*GFRS—Graduate Funding Resource System.* The GFRS has provided computerized access to graduate-level award opportunities since 1977. The database contains more than 2,300 award citations focused specifically on fellowships, grants, and awards for graduate and postdoctoral study and research. Citation references are based on direct responses from awarding organizations. Users not associated with the University of Washington can submit an application form and receive an awards listing. A flat rate of $10 per search is charged.

*SPIN—Sponsored Programs Information Network.* Established in 1980, SPIN is a computerized list of funding opportunities (federal, nonfederal, and corporate) and is designed to assist in the identification of external support for research, education, and development projects. The service was originally developed to aid the State University of New York system faculty. SPIN services are now available by subscription to all colleges and universities across the country.

*CASHE—College Aid Sources for Higher Education.* CASHE, developed by National College Services, Ltd., is a user-friendly, computerized database of financial aid sources containing more than 4,100 sources, 14,000 resources, and 150,000 resources distributions (the total number of awards included in each resource). Begun as an undergraduate database, CASHE now has graduate aid sources as well. CASHE is sold to colleges and universities that make the information available either directly; on-line with National College Services, Ltd., where data are updated daily; or via diskettes updated twice a year. If your school's Financial Aid Office has purchased the CASHE database, by all means take a look at it. Some schools charge a fee of anywhere from $5 to $50 to use the CASHE system on campus.

## Web Sites to Explore

If you have not explored the financial resources on the World Wide Web, your search is not complete. Now available on the Web is a wealth of information ranging from loan and entrance applications to minority grants and scholarships.

**Introduction to the Web.** The Web combines graphic and text information in an easy-to-use environment. Starting with a Web browser like Netscape or Mosaic, which most colleges have on-line, you can access the Web from your college computer center or through an on-line provider service like CompuServe or America Online. Give yourself about an hour or two to become familiar with the Web if it is your first time. Once you're acquainted with it, search for Financial Aid, possibly a subdirectory under Higher Education. Then just point and click through the directories/pages as necessary.

**Web Mailing Lists.** There is a mailing list or news group called "Grants-L" on the Web for announcements of grants and fellowships of interest to graduate students. To subscribe, send your e-mail to: listserve@listproc.gsu.edu. In the body of the mail write "subscribe grants-l". Include your name and e-mail address.

**University-Specific Information on the Web.** University of Florida, Virginia Tech, University of Massachusetts, Emory, and Georgetown University are just a few of the universities that have their own financial aid directories on the Web. If you're interested in a school that has one, you can download admissions applications to start the graduate process. After that, you can obtain detailed information on financial aid processes, forms, and deadlines. You can also find university-specific grant and scholarship information. You may be able to learn more financing information by using the Web than by an actual visit. If you have a question, you can ask on-line.

**Scholarships on the Web.** Dictionary-sized books listing scholarships will probably be obsolete in the future; they will be converted to electronic databases that you will be able to access right on the Web. Right now many benefactors and other scholarship donors are creating pages on the Web that list information about their specific scholarships. You can reach this information through a Web browser, by, for example, searching a topic like Minority Scholarships. New scholarship pages are being added to the Web daily.

The Web also lists many services that, often for a fee, can search for scholarships for you. While some of these might be helpful, surfing the Web yourself and using the traditional library resources on available scholarships is often just as effective—and it will cost you little but your time. Some services such as FastWeb, which is an acronym for financial aid search through the Web, may be free through your university. Check with your Financial Aid Office about getting access to such services.

**Bank and Loan Information on the Web.** Banks and loan servicing centers are creating pages on the Web, making it easier to access loan information on-line. Having the information on screen in front of you instantaneously is more convenient than being put on hold on the phone. And you can find a good deal of information there: interest rate variations, descriptions of loans, loan consolidation programs, and repayment charts can all be found on the Web. One such website is Peterson's Education Center (http://www.petersons.com); visitors can access various lenders and helpful programs.

# THE GRANT APPLICATION: CONVINCING A SPONSOR TO FUND YOU

Once you've defined your project and yourself and have located the proper funding source for your needs, you next have to convince the sponsor to fund you. The vehicle for doing this is the grant application. When you request current information and application forms from the sponsor, the material you receive can vary widely, depending on the type of program, the amount of money, and the type of sponsor. In general, the complexity of the application form varies in direct proportion to the amount of money requested.

The simplest application form is one associated with small awards. In this case, you may merely be asked for standard biographical information—name, address, telephone number, field of study, academic level, academic history, professional or work experience, and financial information.

Sponsors usually also request academic transcripts and letters of recommendation. Sometimes these must be included with the application; in other cases, they must be sent directly by the university or the person providing the recommendation. Most applications ask for at least a short paragraph discussing educational and career plans.

Applying for a larger grant may be more complicated. In addition to the above, you will be asked for a project description averaging two to five pages and for at least a tentative budget. Typically, sponsors want to know:

- how much money you will need
- what you expect to do with it
- how well you have thought out your project
- what your qualifications are for carrying it out successfully
- what is important about your project, both to your program of study and to the field of knowledge to which you will be contributing

You will probably also be asked for letters of recommendation, including one from your faculty adviser or department chair. Major fellowships, such as those from IREX (International Research and Exchanges Board) or the Department of Education (Fulbright-Hays Doctoral Dissertation Research Abroad Program), can provide up to $20,000 or more to cover living expenses, international travel, research costs, allowances for dependents, and more. The sponsors of these awards are justifiably interested in finding out as much about you as possible to help them make informed decisions. Application forms for these awards are much more complicated and typically require the following supporting documents:

- curriculum vitae
- official transcripts
- three letters of recommendation
- documentation of language proficiency
- project description of up to ten pages, including literature review
- budget
- approval of dissertation adviser

All applications, whether for large grants or small awards, however, require the same basic information. With this in mind, you are best advised to apply for many if you're applying for one—this way, you will make better use of your time as well as increase your chances of actually being chosen.

One important thing to remember is that every aspect of your application reflects back on you. Be neat. Never submit a hand-written proposal. If using a printer, make sure your printing format is at least letter quality. While the substance of your proposal will ultimately determine your acceptance or rejection, the style of it will also come into play. A neat, well-formatted proposal conveys professionalism. It tells your sponsor you are mature, capable, well qualified, and in touch with the mechanics of sophisticated interaction. To ensure your application has been received, send a stamped return postcard that your sponsor can simply drop in the mail.

Judith Margolin, in her extremely helpful and clearly presented book *The Individual's Guide to Grants* (New York: Plenum Press, 1987), suggests you view the proposal as "a natural outgrowth of the research you have done, identifying potential funders and learning as much as possible about funders' grant-making policies and preferred procedures for application. If you have done this homework thoroughly, your proposal will seem to write itself."

Most students who have been through the grant-seeking process say that the ease and accuracy with which they completed their application, wrote their proposals, or composed a statement of interest depended directly on how much they knew about the funder's grant-making policies.

## Getting Nominated

About 5 percent of grant programs require that the candidate be nominated. Of these, most specify that the nomination come from a faculty member, adviser, or sponsor. A few require nomination from a graduate dean, the dean of the faculty, or the student's institution. The remaining handful—programs sponsored by professional or honor societies—state that society members must make the nomination.

How do you get nominated? It's easy: You approach the appropriate person with some documentation in hand (for example, a program description, perhaps a short personal statement, an unofficial transcript, or other information) and mention you would like to be considered for nomination. Is this pushy? Maybe so. But if you're not up front about wanting to be nominated, no one will ever know you're interested. This does not, however, ensure you *will* be nominated. It's only a strategy for putting your hat in the ring.

## How Do You Write a Proposal or a Budget?

Proposal writing is an important skill to learn. For those who are considering a career in academia, it may be necessary to fund future research—and even one's job—through a series of grants. Educators and public officials often find themselves writing grant proposals to support new or ongoing programs; the same is true for arts administrators and public service groups. Business people and entrepreneurs are also required to write proposals; in their case, the proposal centers on finding a private source of capital for a start-up enterprise or the creation of a new department. In almost all phases of professional employment, in fact, the ins and outs of proposal writing eventually come into play.

The good news for graduate students is that few grant and fellowship applications require a full-blown proposal (with such components as an abstract, goals and objectives, procedure, and methodology). Most ask merely for a personal statement or essay— usually on the order of 1,000 to 5,000 words describing your academic background, reasons for choosing your field of study, and plans for utilizing the grant award.

But even when you're writing such a brief essay, it's important to be clear, to be professional, and to let your own voice speak. Show what makes you stand out as an individual. If you're enthusiastic about your project, make sure it shows. Real people are going to read what you've written. If your very first sentence catches their attention, so much the better.

One way to pep up personal statements is to avoid the obvious opener: "I first wanted to be a doctor when I went with my father on his hospital rounds." Instead, why not use: "My first exposure to the hard side of medicine came when I was a high school girl watching my father, a cardiosurgeon, deal with a patient in great pain from his open-heart surgery. 'Can't you reduce the pain, doctor?' the young man asked. 'Not without side effects,' my father answered. That's when I realized I wanted to be as gutsy as dad. I wanted to be a surgeon too."

---

## WORK ON THE LEAD

Learning to write well is like learning to play the piano; it takes practice, practice, and more practice. You must go over a piece of prose until it is reasonably smooth. This means drafting and redrafting. It may be tedious but it's essential. Two things to aim for in a personal statement are an arresting, attention-getting lead sentence or paragraph and clarity of expression.

Let's talk about the lead. In a society so exposed to media, you are competing for the grant committee's attention with newspapers, magazines, and sprightly ad copy. We expect all writing to be immediately rewarding. Our boredom threshold is low indeed.

Here's how the Associated Press started a story of an unusual woman: "Colina, Chile—Leontina Albina does not expect much from her children on Mother's Day. She did not raise the 53 of them to be like that."

A *Boston Globe* story started this way: "San Francisco—Last January, there were bad vibes in the Haight-Ashbury area. The merchants and residents were fed up with the trash and litter caused by transients. The Summer of Love had chilled into the Winter of Discontent."

You, too, can write catchy openings. An M.B.A. candidate got his personal statement off to a lively start in this fashion: "You can't know what you don't know. That's why I think I need an M.B.A. Last year, I had to throw in the sponge and file for bankruptcy. I don't want this to ever happen again. For me, an M.B.A. is going to be a form of preventive business medicine."

An applicant for funds to attend a top journalism school opened her personal statement with: "Five years working for a metropolitan daily have taught me one thing: I need time to develop skills I simply can't learn on the job. You can't expect busy editors to drop everything and coach you on your reporting or analyze weaknesses in your copy."

These are not brilliant ideas, but they sure do beat: "I want an M.B.A. in order to learn the accounting procedures necessary for an entrepreneurial success" or "After five years as a member of the working press, it's time for me to take a year off to polish my journalistic skills."

To write a good lead, abandon the chronological account and search for something significant in a sequence of observations you plan to present to the funding committee. Ask yourself "What's important in what I am going to say?" rather than "In what time period should I begin my statement?" If you are proud of earning a Phi Beta Kappa key, you don't begin with a history of all the A's you earned; you begin with the moment you learned you had been invited to join that illustrious fraternity of scholars.

You can easily develop this habit of noticing how reporters develop leads in the newspapers or on television. They seldom respect chronology except in adjunct, sidebar material. They report first that the Iranian Airbus was shot down with a loss of 290 passengers. Not that the crew of the Vincennes spotted something on the radar, hesitated briefly, then fired. That follows later. The lead, the headline, presents the most significant facts, often the "who, what, where, when, and why."

Adapted from: Howard Greene and Robert Minton, *Behind the Ivy Wall*. Boston: Little Brown, 1989

# THE PROPOSAL

The proposal is your chance to present your ideas to the funding source. If you view it as a vehicle for communicating your enthusiasm, the actual writing may come far more easily. It may help to think of your project as a product you are trying to market and the proposal as the packaging. Make the package attractive and appealing so that the sponsor will want to invest in the product.

Many students ask how technical their proposals should be. Generally, the best advice is to avoid jargon as much as possible. Some of the questions to consider when making a decision about the technicality of language are:

- Who will be evaluating the proposal, experts in the particular field or a general fellowship committee? (In many cases this information is available in the information packet provided with grant applications. If not, you should ask when making the original contact.)

- What type of organization is sponsoring the award, a professional organization or a foundation?

- Can you accurately describe your project with a nontechnical vocabulary? Unless you are applying for a grant for which experts in the field review applications (such as a National Science Foundation Award), try to limit your use of technical terms as much as possible. Obviously, this will be easier in some fields than others.

Each of the parts of a proposal serves a purpose. Depending on your field of study, some will be more important than others. The various components from which you will choose are:

- cover letter
- abstract
- summary
- introduction
- objectives
- methods and materials or procedures

- evaluation
- budget
- future funding
- appendix

## The Cover Letter

A cover letter informs the sponsor that you are including a proposal for consideration. Mention the name of the award for which you are applying, state the deadline and the expected announcement date, and give the title of the project. If your proposal contains an abstract, one is not needed here. If not, you can include one in your cover letter. If possible, address the cover letter to a specific person, using the name of the program's contact person or the program administrator. You can get this information by calling the organization's general phone number and asking for the name of the appropriate contact person. Explain that you will be submitting a proposal and wish to address it correctly.

Avoid using the impersonal "Dear Sir or Madam," which suggests you don't know much about the sponsor or haven't done your homework. As a last resort, address your letter to the organization's executive secretary, executive director, or president.

## The Abstract

The abstract is a concise statement of your objectives and procedures. Essentially, it tells the reader in one or two sentences what you plan to do and how. Application forms often provide one inch of space in which to type your abstract, enough for three or four lines of type. Although this is the funder's first contact with your project, it may very well be the last thing you write. It is best to write an abstract after you have completed the rest of your proposal. The abstract is drawn directly from the body of the proposal and distills its essential elements. Omit any unnecessary words or phrases.

The following are a few sample abstracts:

Localization of glucose–6–phosphatase in the endoplasmic of neonatal rat liver will be studied using biochemical and histochemical techniques. The results should shed light on the mechanism by which cell membranes are constructed.

Observation of a troop of the black-and-white Colobus monkey (*colobus abysinnicus*) in the wild will be carried out in an attempt to elucidate the role played by the alpha male in the troop's social organization.

Translation of *La Nouvelle Romance*, the first novel by the Congolese writer and politician Henri Lopes, will introduce the English-language public to this author's perceptive comments on postindependence African society.

## The Summary

A summary is longer than an abstract and can be as much as several pages in length. For a five-page proposal, the abstract can serve as a summary, while a twenty-page proposal would typically require a one-or two-page summary. All the essential elements of the proposal are included in a summary, but in condensed form. It reminds the reader what you are planning to do, why, how, in what time frame, and what your funding needs are.

If a sponsor requires a preliminary proposal, your summary can also serve this purpose. Sponsors who work this way select finalists on the basis of the preliminary submission and invite them to present full-length proposals. If you are trying to find out whether your project falls within the funding guidelines of an organization, you could present your summary for consideration, rather than a complete proposal. Like an abstract, your summary might be written after you have written your longer proposal. On the other hand, it could also serve as an outline to assist you in writing a longer proposal.

## The Introduction

The introduction presents the who and the why behind a project. On one hand, it establishes your credibility—who you are and what your qualifications are for carrying out this particular project. And, on the other hand, it places your project in perspective by summarizing important findings in the field and outlining what needs your project will address. It indicates how your findings will contribute to the body of knowledge and what their broader applications might be. The introduction also establishes a link between your work and the stated interests of the sponsor.

## Objectives

This section of a proposal describes in a very precise way what your hypotheses are and what you hope to accomplish. Your project may have one single objective or more than one. Objectives are outcomes that can be evaluated at the end of the project. Your objective might be, for example, to increase the number of women using a family-planning service, or you could be attempting to clarify the economic conditions underlying the fall of the Marcos government in the Philippines. If applicable, your objectives should define the population group affected by your work.

## Methods and Materials or Procedures

The methods section describes in detail how and where you plan to carry out your objectives. What sort of data will you collect, and how will you go about getting it? What criteria will you use to select your sample populations? How will you design your experiments? How will subjects be chosen and questioned? This is the section to address the issues related to your methodology.

## Evaluation

Every proposed project should have some method for evaluation built into it. The evaluation section describes the methods and criteria for measuring the project's success in meeting its objectives. Success can be either procedural—were the procedures adequate and well designed?—or substantive—are the results significant? Your evaluation may look at whether the data collected are representative, how results were analyzed, and how and to whom they were disseminated. Evaluation could, for example, include the publication of a book as a result of your work or the presentation of an art exhibit.

## The Budget

The budget presents to the sponsor in a clear and well-thought-out manner what your projected expenses are and how they will be met. Your budget should be reasonable (i.e., proportional to the scope and significance of the project). Try to estimate expenses as closely as possible. Don't pad your budget; every item should be justified by your procedures. On the other hand, don't be overly frugal. For example, a project to conduct a survey could include costs for the printing and mailing of questionnaires, the services of a typist, some travel, and the use of a computer to analyze the responses, including the cost of specialized software.

A major additional expense is the time you invested conducting the project, that is, your expenses. All these items should be included in the budget. A complete balance sheet might look like that found in the table on the next page.

The budget should clearly display the total projected expenses of the project—those for which you are requesting funds from the sponsor plus those for which support is expected from elsewhere. Depending on your budget, you may also need to budget for evaluation if, for example, you plan to survey participants after the project is completed. If you are

**127**

requesting money for living expenses (your salary), you will have to calculate as precisely as possible what your actual living expenses would be. If you solicit travel funds, base your calculations on ticket prices quoted by a travel agent. Remember that a detailed, accurate budget reflects careful thinking and gives a good impression of the applicant.

## Sample Budget for Grant Application

| Expenses | Funds Requested from Sponsor | Funds Provided by Others | In-Kind Contributions | Totals |
|---|---|---|---|---|
| Personnel salary, project director (student) half-time, 6 months, based on $12,000 yr. full-time | | | $3000 | $3000 |
| salary, typist: 20 hrs. @ $6 hr. | $120 | | | $120 |
| personal printing: 100 questionnaires | $250 | $250 | | |
| postage: 1,000 x .32 | $320 | | $320 | |
| travel: 300 mi. @.22 mi. | $66 | | | $66 |
| computer time: 50 hrs. @ $10 hr. | | $500 (university) | | $500 |
| Subtotals | $756 | $500 | $3,000 | $4,256 |

Source: *Grants for Graduate Study*, 3rd edition. Princeton, N.J.: Peterson's Guides, 1992.

# The Appendix

You may be requested to provide supporting material as an appendix to your proposal. The instructions for some programs are very specific regarding what is required and what is precluded. Follow the directions to the letter. If no relevant instructions are provided, either contact the sponsor for guidance or use your best judgment. You may choose to include some documentation as a way to strengthen your application. In addition to curriculum vitae, letters of recommendation, and transcripts, you could include reviews of your work; letters from editors or publishers; a list of prizes, grants, fellowships, and honors; writing samples; a list of publications; slides of your creative work; or tapes of your music. Include whatever would build your case, but be reasonable. A large appendix can discourage the reviewer from looking at any of it.

# ELEMENTS OF A SUCCESSFUL PROPOSAL

A successful proposal establishes a strong link between the applicant's interests and those of the sponsor by presenting a creative approach to an interesting problem. Bruce McCandless, Director of the Office of Research Affairs at the University of Massachusetts at Amherst, defines a successful proposal as "being in the right place at the right time with a convincing case that you are promoting the sponsor's interest."

But how can you build a successful case? One way is to match it to the following list of successful elements.

Does it:

- address a significant problem?
- define specific objectives?
- use a creative, innovative approach?
- detail well-conceived methods?
- request funds in proportion to the scope of the project?
- assure the sponsor that the applicant is well qualified to bring the project to a successful conclusion?
- flow logically?
- meet the application deadline?

Is it:

- appropriate to the interests of the sponsor?
- documented well?
- written clearly?
- well thought out?

Writing a good proposal is similar to writing a good term paper. Much of the same advice applies. When you write, visualize a person reading your proposal. Your aim is to communicate to the reader. State things as clearly and simply as possible. A writing teacher once said, "Tell 'em what you're gonna tell 'em, tell 'em, and tell 'em what you told them."

Prepare your reader for your ideas, present your ideas in a straightforward manner, and then briefly recapitulate. What are your main ideas? Can your reader identify the focus point? Your ideas should stand out and not be camouflaged by supplementary thoughts. Get to the points. Don't dance around them. Be as forceful as you can. Begin with a strong opening statement, and end with a strong conclusion.

If you're having trouble writing, you might try either of Natalie Goldberg's books, *Writing Down the Bones* (Boston: Shambhala, 1986), or *Wild Mind* (New York: Bantam/New Age Books, 1990). Goldberg's advice is simple: First put down all your thoughts without editing. Place the pen on the paper or your fingers on the keyboard and just write without stopping. Time yourself—10 minutes, 20 minutes. Take the whole time. Don't go back or stop to think. In this way, she says, you will "burn through" to first thoughts instead of always writing in carefully edited phrases. Don't edit at this stage, just write. Get all your ideas on paper or screen before you begin to weed them out or refine them.

---

## Elements of an Unsuccessful Proposal

---

The following are some of the common weaknesses of rejected proposals:

- unrelated to the interests of the sponsor
- research uninteresting or unimportant
- project not original
- objectives unclear
- methods not appropriate to objectives
- applicant not qualified or qualifications not specified
- budget inappropriate to scope of project
- budget not within funding range of sponsor
- too complicated
- not well explained
- uses too much technical jargon
- sponsor does not fund individuals (or students)
- proposal does not follow format specified by sponsor
- requested supporting documents not provided
- proposal submitted after deadline

# WHAT TO DO IF YOU SUCCEED— OR FAIL

If your application is accepted and you are awarded money, rejoice! Notify your adviser and your department chair. Send a note to the office on campus that handles grants and fellowships. Find out if there are any bonuses attached to being awarded a grant or fellowship. For example, your university may provide a partial tuition waiver if you bring in more than an established minimum of money. Write a letter to the sponsor explaining your plans to begin the proposed project and expressing thanks for the grant. Then congratulate yourself for a job well done and get on with your work.

---

## A SAMPLING OF SUCCESS RATES

The following are figures representative of the general success ratio for grant requests:

- The National Science Foundation Graduate Research Fellows Program awarded 760 fellowships out of 5,367 applicants in fiscal year 1988 (14 percent).
- The National Science Foundation Minority Graduate Fellows Program funded 100 out of 797 applicants in 1988 (12.5 percent).
- The Population Council awarded 19 fellowships out of 241 applicants in 1988 (8 percent).
- The National Gallery of Art funded 9 out of 97 applicants in 1988 (9 percent).

Source: *Grants for Graduate Study*, 3rd edition. Princeton, N.J.: Peterson's Guides, 1992.

---

If, on the other hand, your application is turned down, don't despair. It happens to the best and most experienced researchers. In fact, on the average, only 10–30 percent of all proposals are funded, which means that 70-90 percent fail. Funds are scarce, but there are basketsful of good projects. Being rejected doesn't necessarily mean your idea was not good or that you are not well qualified. Remember to look on the grant-seeking process as an element of your education. Make use of your failure to try to improve your chances of future success.

You might be able to get feedback from the sponsor about why your proposal was turned down, which can help you prepare more successful proposals. If proposals are formally reviewed, reviewers are usually asked to submit written comments to the selection committee. Address a polite letter to the sponsor stating your disappointment at not being funded. Mention that you would appreciate receiving a copy of the reviewers' comments to help you modify your proposal and possibly resubmit it later. You might also ask whether it was felt that your project fell outside the scope of the program or if the sponsor could provide any suggestions for improvement. The advice you receive might be helpful. Some organizations, however, are not in a position to provide you with feedback. In that case, you might choose to discuss the proposal with your adviser or a grants office on campus.

Every researcher who has been successfully funded has also experienced rejection at least once. One best-selling novel was offered to thirty publishers before it was finally accepted. Don't give up. If at first you don't succeed, apply, apply again.

# SOURCES OF GRANT SUPPORT

Anyone who has ever gone to the library or browsed the Internet to look up sources of foundation or corporate support for graduate study knows that it's best to allot at least a few days to the effort. There are literally *thousands* of entries in dozens of books and references detailing individual organizations and the awards they have chosen to sponsor. In the section that follows, you'll be introduced to some of the many grants available. Keep in mind as you read this section that the list of grants described here is not comprehensive; it is merely as sampling of some of the organizations that offer general grant support to graduate students.

**Flemish Community**
This is a grant/scholarship award for any field of graduate study to students of Flemish heritage. Funds may be used for research costs, living expenses, tuition and fees, support for spouse/dependents, books, language course, printing of thesis or dissertation. Five awards are offered each year. In the most recent award period, there were fifteen applicants. The award is renewable and varies in amount.

Applicants must be college seniors or B.A./B.S. holders and no more than 35 years old. Recipients are selected on the basis of academic achievement and quality of proposed research. U.S. citizenship is required. The application form is available year-round from the address below. Applications are due March 1; recipients are announced in July.

*Contact:* Rita Omwal
Attache of the Flemish Community
Flemish Community Graduate Studies Grant
Flemish Community c/o Embassy of Belgium
3330 Garfield Street, NW
Washington, D.C. 20008
202-333-6900 Ext. 231

### Honor Society of Phi Kappa Phi

This is a fellowship award for any field of graduate study. Funds may be used for living expenses, tuition and fees, or travel costs. Eighty awards are offered once a year. In the most recent award period, there were 183 applicants. Award values range from $1,000 to $7,000.

Applicants must be graduating college seniors or B.A./B.S. holders. Recipients are selected on the basis of academic achievement (top 10 percent of their classes) and must be members of the Honor Society of Phi Kappa Phi. Applicants must be nominated by their universities chapters. Application forms are available October 1 from the address below. They are due March 1, and recipients are announced April 15.

*Contact:* Dr. John W. Warren, Executive Director
Phi Kappa Phi Graduate Fellowships
Honor Society of Phi Kappa Phi
Louisiana State University
P.O. Box 16000
Baton Rouge, LA 70893–1410
504-388-4917

### Houghton Mifflin Company

This is a fellowship award for any field of graduate study. Funds may be used for any purpose desired by recipient. Awards are offered once a year and are not renewable. The award value is $10,000.

There are no restrictions on the academic level of the applicant. Recipients are selected on the basis of quality of writing and publishability. U.S. citizenship required. Applications accepted continuously, and announcements are made as awards are given.

*Contact:* Janice Harvey, Submissions Editor
Houghton Mifflin Literary Fellowship
Houghton Mifflin Co.
2 Park Street
Boston, MA 02108–4894
617-725–5900

**133**

## Kosciuszko Foundation

This is a grant/scholarship award for any field of graduate study. Funds may be used for living expenses or travel costs. The award offers a stipend and tuition remission. Awards are offered once a year and are not renewable.

The value varies according to your program of study. It is preferred that applicants be doctoral candidates. They must be of Polish heritage residing in the U.S. Application forms are available from the address below and are due November 15.

*Contact:* Kosciuszko Foundation
15 East 65th Street
New York, NY 10021
212-734-2130

## Marshall Aid Commemoration Commission

This is a grant/scholarship award for any field of graduate study. Funds may be used for research costs, living expenses, tuition and fees, travel costs, or support for spouse/dependents. There are forty awards offered once a year. In the most recent award period, there were 800 applicants. The award is renewable.

Applicants must be college seniors or B.A./B.S. holders who have not reached their 26th birthday by October 1. Recipients are selected on the basis of academic achievement (minimum 3.7 GPA), quality of proposed research, and personal qualities. Unmarried applicants are preferred. Application forms are available June 30 from address below and are due October 16. Recipients are announced in early December.

*Contact:* British Marshall Scholarships
Marshall Aid Commemoration Commission
Cultural Department, British Embassy
3100 Massachusetts Avenue, NW
Washington, D.C. 20008-3600
202-462-1340

## National Collegiate Athletic Association

This is a grant/scholarship award for any field of graduate study. Funds may be used for living expenses or tuition and fees. Awards are offered three times a year and are valued at $4,000.

Applicants must be in the last year of intercollegiate athletic competition under NCAA regulation. Recipients are selected on the basis of academic achievement (minimum 3.0 GPA) and athletic achievement. The applicant must be a student athlete at an NCAA-member institution and must be nominated by a faculty athletics representative or by the director of athletics. Application forms are available in September, February, and April from address below and are due October, April, and May; announcements are made continuously.

*Contact:* Fannie Vaughan, Executive Assistant
NCAA Postgraduate Scholarship Program
National Collegiate Athletic Association
P.O. Box 1906
Mission, KS 66201
913-384-3220

### Northwood Institute Alden B. Dow Creativity Center
This is a residential fellowship for any field of graduate study. Funds may be used for research costs, living expenses, travel costs, or project costs. There are four awards offered once a year.

There are no restrictions based on the academic level of the applicant. Recipients are selected on the basis of proposed research. Application forms are available from the address below and are due December 31. Recipients are announced April 1.

*Contact:* Carol B. Coppage, Director
Creativity Fellowships
Northwood Institute Alden B. Dow Creativity Center
Midland, MI 48640–2398

### Omega Psi Phi Fraternity, Inc.
This is a grant/scholarship award for any field of graduate study. Funds may be used for study in graduate or professional school. Awards are offered once a year and are worth up to $500.

Applicants must be B.A./B.S. holders, men, and members of Omega Psi Phi Fraternity, Inc. Recipients are selected on the basis of academic achievement and financial need. Application forms are available from the address below and are due May 15.

*Contact:* Undergraduate and Graduate Scholarship Grants
Omega Psi Phi Fraternity, Inc.
Drew Scholarship Commission
2714 Georgia Avenue NW
Washington, D.C. 20001
202-667-7158

### Rotary Foundation of Rotary International
The Rotary Foundation offers several types of international scholarship opportunities, including the following:

- Academic-Year Ambassadorial Scholarships provide funding for one academic year of study in another country. This award is intended to help cover round-trip transportation, tuition, fees, room and board, and miscellaneous expenses of up to $22,000 (U.S.) or its equivalent.

- Multi-Year Ambassadorial Scholarships are for either two or three years of degree-oriented study in another country. A flat grant of $11,000 (U.S.) or its equivalent is provided per year to be applied toward the cost of a degree program.

- Cultural Ambassadorial Scholarships are for either three or six months of intensive language study and cultural immersion in another country and provide funds to cover round-trip transportation, tuition, fees, room, board, and miscellaneous expenses up to $10,000 (U.S.) and $17,000 (U.S.), respectively. Applications will be considered for candidates interested in studying Arabic, English, French, German, Hebrew, Italian, Japanese, Mandarin Chinese, Polish, Portuguese, Russian, Spanish, Swahili, and Swedish.

Note that not all Rotary districts are able to offer ambassadorial scholarships every year. Students are encouraged to contact the Rotary Club nearest them regarding local deadlines, the availability of the specific scholarships outlined above, and application material. Since application material will be delivered no earlier than November, contact your local Rotary Club in November/December.

*Contact:* Margaret Omori
Supervisor of Rotary Foundation Scholarships
Rotary Foundation of Rotary International
One Rotary Center
1560 Sherman Avenue
Evanston, IL 60201
708-866-3000

### Hattie M. Strong Foundation
This is an interest-free loan for any field of graduate study. Funds may be used for research costs, living expenses, tuition and fees, travel costs, secretarial/research assistance, or support for spouse/dependents. From 200 to 250 awards are offered once a year. In the most recent award period, there were 570 applicants. Award values range from $1,000 to $2,500.

Applicants must be B.A./B.S. holders, U.S. citizens, and within one year of completing degree program. Recipients are selected on the basis of academic achievement, financial need, and character. Application forms are available January 1 from the address below and are due March 31. Recipients are announced in June or July.

*Contact:* Barbara B. Cantrell
Director of Loans
Hattie M. Strong Foundation
1735 I Street, NW, Suite 705
Washington, D.C. 20006
202-331-1619

### Josephine de Karman Fellowship Trust

This is a fellowship award for any field of graduate study. Funds may be used for any purpose decided upon by the recipient. Ten awards valued at $6,000 are made each year.

Applicants must be entering the terminal year of graduate school. Special consideration is given those studying in the humanities. Application forms are available until January 15 from the address listed below and are due January 31. Award announcements are made by April 15.

*Contact:* Lucy Hays, Secretary
Fellowship Committee
Josephine de Karman Fellowship Trust
1069 Via Verde, Suite 217
San Dimas, CA 91773

While the above are all examples of foundation or corporate support for graduate work in any field of study, the following two awards are examples of funding for specific fields of study.

### Howard Hughes Medical Institute Doctoral Fellowships in Biological Science

This is a fellowship award with the purpose of supporting the education of outstanding prospective investigators to ensure the strength and vigor of the scientific pool for biomedical research. It is for study in cell biology and regulation, genetics, immunology, neuroscience, and structural biology. It is a $14,500 stipend plus up to $14,000 for tuition and fees for three years.

Applicants must be B.A./B.S. holders and enrolled in a program related to the fields listed above. Applications are available from the address listed below. The deadline is November 3, and awards are announced in April.

*Contact:* Hughes Predoctoral Fellowships
The Fellowship Office
National Research Council
2101 Constitution Avenue, NW
Washington, D.C. 20418
202-334-2872

**American Sociological Association Minority Fellowship Program**
This is a fellowship award with the purpose of contributing to the development of sociology by recruiting persons who will add differing orientations and creativity to the field. Its value is $10,000 plus full or partial tuition.

The award is open to citizens or permanent residents of the U.S. pursuing a Ph.D. in sociology. Applicants must be members of an underrepresented racial or ethnic group. Applicants must document an interest in and commitment to teaching, research, and service careers on the sociological aspects of mental health issues of ethnic and racial minorities. Applications are available from the address listed below. The deadline is December 31.

*Contact:* American Sociological Association
Minority Fellowship Program
1722 N Street, NW
Washington, D.C. 20036
202-822-3410

Many such field-specific awards can be located by researching the various funding source books and databases that are listed in the Appendices. And don't forget to search the Web for the wealth of information available there.

# FINANCIAL AID FOR SPECIFIC STUDENT GROUPS

I f you are an international student planning to study in the United States, an American wanting to study abroad, a woman, a member of a minority group, or a veteran, take note. This chapter is devoted to funding information for you.

## INTERNATIONAL STUDENTS AT U.S. GRADUATE SCHOOLS

Almost three-quarters of the international students studying at U.S. graduate schools receive their funding from sources outside the United States: 65 percent from personal or family sources, and about 8 percent from their home governments.

Of the 25 percent of international students who receive money from this country, the most significant source is the graduate school itself. Colleges and universities provide primary funding to nearly 18 percent of the international students who attend American graduate schools. Another 3 percent get their primary funding from private sponsors in this country—nonprofit organizations, foundations, corporations, and a variety of other agencies. And the U.S. government is the primary source of support for about another 3 percent of these students.

In general, funding of international students has become a source of controversy among Americans who lack the necessary funds to pursue higher education. "All I know is that the government's constantly slashing funds for our own citizens to pursue graduate and postgraduate education," says one student. "But here you have growing numbers of foreign students who are lured to this country by a government that places more emphasis on diplomacy than on the development of its own national talent pool."

Others, however, see the growing number of international students funded with U.S. money as an investment. "It's another form of foreign aid," says an economist with the American International Foundation. "We give money to countries for all kinds of reasons having to do with raising their standards of living. This is just another attempt to provide other countries with a talent pool of their own. And if these students wind up staying here, then they're part of our talent pool."

## Where to Seek Help

It is advisable to begin your search for aid by contacting the U.S. educational advising center in your home country. Since these centers maintain contact with U.S. colleges and universities, they know which American institutions are committed to funding international education and which universities are research institutions. They will also be able to help you distinguish among schools on the basis of cost.

## The Challenge of Finding Funding

Students who are neither citizens nor permanent residents of the United States are considered international students. Usually these students are in the United States on either an F-1 or J-1 visa and must return to their home countries upon completion of studies. The search for financial aid funding sources is particularly difficult for these international students who do not qualify for the loans and work-study programs offered by the U.S. government.

Regrettably, financial assistance for international students is, indeed, limited. As a general rule, international undergraduate students do not receive any assistance from their colleges or universities. But some academic departments may offer graduate student support. Listed below are programs that are available to international students.

## Sources of Funding for International Students

The types of aid available to international students range from grants to fellowships to scholarships to internships to assistantships to residencies. There is also a wide range of types of sponsor organizations—colleges and universities, private foundations, corporations, and government bodies. *Funding for U.S. Study—A Guide for Foreign Nationals*, compiled by the Institute of International Education, 809 United Nations

Plaza, New York, New York 10017-3580, lists many fellowships for international students studying in the United States. Its phone number is 212-883-8200.

See Appendix E for publications that provide information on financial assistance programs—both public and private—for international students.

## Loans

With a U.S. citizen as cosigner, international students may be eligible to borrow through private loan programs such as the SHARE and GradSHARE programs offered by Nellie Mae or the programs offered by TERI, The Educational Resources Institute. Information about these programs is available through your graduate school's Financial Aid Office or by calling Nellie Mae at 800-634-9308 or TERI at 800-255-TERI.

## Work

During the first year of study, international students are eligible to work only on campus in jobs that relate to their programs of study. After their first year of study, they are eligible to work both on and off campus. International students in graduate programs are eligible to receive graduate assistantships and interested students should contact their graduate school's dean's office.

---

# AVOIDING FINANCIAL DIFFICULTIES

Financial difficulties are undoubtedly the most common, persistent problem facing international students studying in the United States. Students who have full and continuing sponsorship from private or public sources can sail through their education without worrying about finances. But many students—perhaps the majority—face financial problems at some time or another, and must seek alternative ways to continue their studies.

Student advisers and others on campus who work with international students on a daily basis have seen a whole spectrum of problems—from temporary situations in which short-term emergency loans are enough to solve a student's difficulties, to situations in which students become destitute. While U.S. advisers are generally very willing to work with students who face adversity, they lament the fact that many problems could be anticipated before students arrive.

What kinds of financial problems do international students face? Here are some of the common ones:

- Economic problems in the home country forced the government to devalue the currency. Now the sponsor must come up with more money in the country's currency to buy the same number of dollars.
- Because of economic problems, the government will now allow only a certain amount of money to be sent abroad to each student ($9,000, for example) and that is not enough to cover the student's expenses.
- The student has a scholarship to study in the United States, but for any one of several possible reasons it has been reduced or canceled entirely.
- The student's sponsor died or suffered a business reversal that affects the amount of money that can be sent to the student.
- Family circumstances have changed. A sibling is now entering a university and also needs financial support, or a member of the family is ill and needs medical attention.
- The student has become ill or has had an accident not entirely covered by medical insurance and has had to use money that was intended to pay for tuition or living expenses for medical bills.
- There has been inadequate support for the student from the beginning.
- The student miscalculated the cost of education. People who have never been to the United States sometimes cannot believe the estimated costs quoted by colleges and universities. They believe they can do it on much less.
- Students sometimes secure only the first year of funding, hoping the rest will magically "turn up."
- Many students think they can send money home from their monthly stipends. When they try to do so, they experience a shortage in terms of their educational needs.

How can these pitfalls be avoided? People who work with international students on a daily basis have reached the conclusion that if students do not have adequate financial support, they should not come to the United States to study. It is a conclusion that students and their families often do not want to hear and one they find difficult to accept. Students should resist the temptation to think that funds will turn up; that they just need to economize and spend money carefully in order to stretch their funds to the needed amount; or even that, because there are so many rich Americans, one will surface with a blank check in hand.

Careful financial planning and budgeting are crucial to the achievement of an educational goal. A realistic plan can make the difference between a productive U.S. academic experience and a return home without a longed-for academic degree.

Adapted from "How to Avoid the Most Common Problems of International Students," Barry Bem, Director, International Student Services, Howard University, given at the Graduate and Professional School Financial Aid Service Workshop in Washington, D.C., in February, 1992.

# U.S. CITIZENS STUDYING ABROAD

There are several different sources of funding for U.S. citizens wishing to study abroad. The Institute for International Education (IIE) publishes a free pamphlet, "Financial Resources for International Study: A Selected Bibliography," that is an excellent reference tool for locating directories listing sources of support for graduate study (see address below).

Another such agency is the Council on International Educational Exchange, 205 East 42nd Street, New York, New York 10017, which publishes *The Student Travel Catalogue*. This publication lists fellowship sources and contains a detailed explanation of the council's services both for American students traveling abroad and for international students interested in coming to the United States to study.

### Institute of International Education (IIE)

IIE offers study/research awards for any field of graduate study to be used abroad. Funds may be used for research costs, living expenses, tuition and fees, travel costs, secretarial/research assistance, or support for spouse/dependents. Approximately 600 nine-month renewable awards of varying value are given. In the most recent award period there were 3,000 applicants.

Applicants must be B.A./B.S. holders and U.S. citizens. Recipients are selected on the basis of academic achievement and quality of the proposed research. Application forms are available May 1 and due October 31; recipients are announced June 1.

*Contact:* Fulbright Grants for Graduate Study or Research Abroad
Institute of International Education
U.S. Student Programs Division
809 United Nations Plaza
New York, NY 10017-3580
212-984-5330

## Federal Funds for Study Abroad

The U.S. Department of Education administers programs under Title VI of the Higher Education Act that support over 700 fellowships related to international education and world area studies.

**Foreign Language and Area Studies Fellowship Program (FLAS)**
This merit-based financial aid program was established to promote a wider knowledge and understanding of other countries and cultures. Schools apply to the Department of Education for FLAS funding in particular world areas. Awards are made to students in language and area studies. Fellowships consist of tuition grants plus a stipend of $7,000. Schools can renew student awards for up to four years.

Applicants must be U.S. citizens. Schools administer the FLAS program on their campuses and set application deadlines and award notification dates.

**Fulbright-Hays Doctoral Dissertation Awards**
Part of Title VI of the Higher Education Act, these awards, known as the Fulbright-Hays Doctoral Dissertation Fellowships, support approximately ninety students each year. Six-month to one-year stipends are awarded to students for doctoral dissertation research. Awards are given for all world areas except Western Europe. Award values range from $5,000 to $55,000, depending on the cost of living in the area of study.

Students must be U.S. citizens and in the dissertation phase of their doctoral programs. Schools must request application materials from the U.S. Department of Education by July and distribute them to their students. The student application deadline is late October or early November; awards are confirmed in late June, although fellows are often notified earlier. The Graduate School names a Fulbright Coordinator on campus. This person should be consulted for more information on these awards.

**USIA Fulbright Fellowships (IIE)**
The federal appropriation, along with support from host countries, is approximately $5 million. Approximately 500 students are supported each year. This program is funded through the U.S. Information Agency (USIA) and administered by the Institute of International Education (IIE) in New York. Fellowships are for one year of study abroad. Award values vary from $2,000 to $26,000, depending on the cost of living in the area of study.

Applicants must be U.S. citizens. The application deadline is October 31; awards are finalized by the end of June. As with the

Fulbright-Hays awards, schools name a fellowship coordinator to administer this program. The coordinator at your school should be consulted for more information.

See Appendix D for publications that provide information on financial assistance programs—both public and private—for U.S. citizens studying abroad.

# MINORITY STUDENTS

Despite recently recorded increases in their rate of high school graduation, ethnic minorities continue to be underrepresented at the undergraduate and, hence, the graduate level. While this generally means fewer opportunities for minority groups as a whole, it also means new opportunities for qualified individuals within those groups. Minority students are in ever greater demand by graduate programs.

## Financial Aid Programs for Minorities

Many factors come into play when discussing the underrepresentation of minority students in graduate programs. Chief among them is the lack of funding many minority students face. For its part, the federal government has established a variety of aid programs designed to help boost the graduate enrollment of minorities. For example, the Patricia Roberts Harris Fellowship, discussed in Chapter 3, is one of the federal Title IX graduate fellowships awarded to underrepresented students. Following are other programs geared for minority graduate students.

### Indian Fellowship Program, U.S. Department of Education
Grant support is available for Native American students enrolled in degree-granting accredited colleges and universities. The value varies and is based on financial need.

Applicants must be persons of one-fourth or more American Indian heritage who are members of tribes for which the federal government has trust responsibility. Deadlines vary.

*Contact:* Home Agency, American Indian Scholarships Inc.
P.O. Box 1106
Taos, NM 87571
or
Grants & Contracts Services
U.S. Department of Education, ACC
600 Independence Avenue, SW

ROB-3, Room 3633
Washington, D.C. 20202-4337
202-708-8228

## Minority Access to Research Careers (MARC)

This program provides support for research training leading to the Ph.D. degree in the biomedical sciences. The awards are for tuition and an annual stipend of $8,500 for up to five years. Applicants must be U.S. citizens or permanent residents who are Native Americans, African Americans, Hispanic Americans, or Pacific Islanders. Recipients must have participated in a MARC Honors Undergraduate Research Training Program and be admitted to a graduate school. The deadline is January 10.

*Contact:* MARC
National Institutes of General Medical Sciences
National Institutes of Health
Bethesda, MD 20892
301-594-3900

## National Aeronautics and Space Administration (NASA)

NASA has an underrepresented minority focus designed to increase minority participation in graduate study, research, and, ultimately, in space science and aerospace technology careers. The award includes a $16,000 stipend, a $3,000 student allowance for expenses, and $3,000 to the university.

Applicants must be U.S. citizens and members of minority groups. Students may enter the program at any time during graduate work or may apply prior to receiving their baccalaureate degrees. Application deadline is February 1; awards are announced by April 15.

*Contact:* NASA Headquarters
Code FEH
300 E Street, NW
Washington, D.C. 20546
202-358–1526

## National Science Foundation Minority Graduate Fellowships

The goal of this program is to improve the human resource base of science and engineering in the United States and to increase the number of practicing scientists and engineers who are members of ethnic minority groups that have traditionally been underrepresented in the advanced levels of the nation's science and engineering talent pool. For students in good standing, awards are available for three years.

The awards provide $8,600 toward the cost of tuition and required fees. (The institution must pay the remaining tuition in the form of a grant.) The annual stipend is $14,400 plus a $1,000 travel stipend.

Applicants must be members of one of the following ethnic minority groups: Native American, African American, Hispanic American, Native Alaskan, or Pacific Islander, and be planning to study engineering, natural sciences, social sciences, or the history and philosophy of science. Two different fellowship programs have also been created to encourage women to undertake graduate study in engineering and computers. U.S. citizens or permanent residents of the United States are eligible to apply. Applicants must not have completed, by the beginning of the fall term, more than 30 semester hours, 45 quarter hours, or the equivalent in supported fields. The application deadline is early November; awards are announced by mid-March. The fellowship competition is administered by the National Research Council.

*Contact:* NSF Graduate Research Fellowship Program
Oak Ridge Associated Universities
P.O. Box 3010
Oak Ridge, TN 37831-3010
423-241-4300

## Privately Sponsored Grants for Minorities

In addition to federal programs specifically geared for minority students, there are also a number of foundation and corporate sponsors eager to increase the visibility of minorities on the graduate level. The following is a list of some of these support sources:

### American Fund for Dental Health

The maximum award amount is $2,000. Applicants must be Native American, African American, Mexican American, or Puerto Rican and must have been accepted at an accredited dental school. The deadline is May 1.

*Contact:* Dental School of the American Fund for Dental Health
211 East Chicago Avenue, Suite 820
Chicago, IL 60611
312-787-6270

## American Geological Institute

The award amount is unspecified. Applicants must be African-American, Hispanic American, or Native American graduate students majoring in geoscience, including geology, geophysics, hydrology, or meteorology. The deadline is February 1.

*Contact:* AGI Minority Participation Program
American Geological Institute
4220 King Street
Alexandria, VA 22302
703-379-2480

## American Planning Association

Annual fellowships range from $2,000 to $5,000. Applicants must be African-American, Mexican-American, Native American, or Puerto Rican graduate students with financial need and must be enrolled in a planning program accredited by the Planning Accreditation Board. Preference is given to full-time students. Students must submit with their applications a two-to five-page personal statement describing why they have chosen planning as a career and how graduate education will be applied to career goals. The deadline is May 15.

*Contact:* APA Planning Fellowship Program
Attn: Assistant for Division and Student Services
American Planning Association
1776 Massachusetts Avenue, NW
Washington, D.C. 20036
202-872-0611

## American Political Science Association

The American Political Science Association Minority Fellowships were established to increase the number of minority Ph.D.'s in political science. Award amounts vary. Applicants must be African-American, Chicano, or Latino political science graduate students with financial need. Applications must be received prior to December 1.

*Contact:* American Political Science Association
1527 New Hampshire Avenue, NW
Washington, D.C. 20036
202-833-3410

## American Sociological Association

Ten fellowships are available, each carrying a maximum stipend of $6,552 per year. Applicants must be African-American, Hispanic

American, Native American, or Asian-American graduate sociology students interested in mental health issues relating to minorities. The deadline is January 15.

*Contact:* American Sociological Association
Minority Fellowship Program
1722 N Street, NW
Washington, D.C. 20036
202-833-3410

### Asian American Journalists Association Award

This program gives awards to outstanding Asian-American students pursuing a career in print, broadcast, or photo journalism. The amount of the awards is up to $2,000. Applicants must be of Asian-American descent and must have a commitment to the Asian-American community, financial need, and personal references. The deadline is April 15.

*Contact:* Asian American Journalist Association Scholarship Committee
1765 Sutter Street, Room 1000
San Francisco, CA 94115
415-346-2051

### The Boston Links

This award is for amounts ranging from $800 to $1,000. Applicants must be African-American graduate students with financial need who are legal residents of the greater Boston area or who attended school in Boston while growing up in the area. The deadline is March 15.

*Contact:* The Boston Links, Inc.
Scholarship for African American Students
5 Wilhelmina Avenue
Burlington, MA 01803

### Committee on Institutional Cooperation (CIC)

The Committee on Institutional Cooperation (CIC), an academic consortium of the "Big Ten" universities and the University of Chicago, offers full tuition and a stipend for minority students to attend one of the CIC institutions. Applicants must be U.S. citizens, members of a minority group, and B.A./B.S. holders.

*Contact:* Ronald Smith, Director
CIC Minorities Fellowship Program
Indiana University
Bloomington, IN 50512
800-457-4420

## Cooperative Research Fellowship Program for Minorities

This award is for tuition and a monthly stipend. Applicants must be members of minority groups beginning graduate work in chemistry, research, physics, or statistics. The deadline varies; applications can be obtained from the address listed below.

*Contact:*  Administrator
Cooperative Research Fellowship Program for Minorities
Room HL-IC 101A
AT&T Bell Laboratories
101 John F. Kennedy Parkway
Short Hills, NJ 07078
201-564-2000

## Ford Foundation Fellowships

This is a fellowship program designed to increase the presence of underrepresented minorities on the nation's college and university faculties. Fellowships are renewable and can be used at any accredited nonprofit United States institution of higher education offering Ph.D.'s and Sc.D.'s in eligible fields. Awards are available for study in research-based doctoral programs in the behavioral and social sciences, humanities, engineering, mathematics, physical sciences, and biological sciences or for interdisciplinary programs comprised of two or more eligible disciplines.

Predoctoral awards provide an annual stipend of $12,000 to the fellow for each of three years of fellowship tenure and an annual institutional grant of $6,000 to the fellowship institution in lieu of tuition and fees. Additionally, the Ford Foundation will provide a $1,000 grant to the undergraduate department of each fellow to be used by the department to encourage minority students to consider graduate study and academic careers.

Dissertation fellowships are available for a twelve-month period. Fellows with previous fellowship support cannot begin Ford Fellowship tenure until their previous fellowship support has ended. Dissertation fellows receive a stipend of $18,000.

Individuals of demonstrated ability who are members of minority groups that have been underrepresented among the disciplines supported by this program are eligible. Applicants must be U.S. citizens or nationals of the United States at the time of application and a member of one of the following groups: Alaskan Natives (Eskimo or Aleut), Native Americans, African Americans, Mexican Americans (Chicanos), Native

Pacific Islanders (Polynesian or Micronesian), and Puerto Ricans. The application deadline is early November.

*Contact:* Ford Foundation Predoctoral and Dissertation Fellowships
for Minorities
Fellowship Office, TJ 2039
National Research Council
2101 Constitution Avenue
Washington, D.C. 20418
202-334-2872
E-mail: infofell@nas.edu
Internet: http://www.nas.edu/fo/index.html

### International Business Machines (IBM) Fellowship

This is a fellowship award for graduate students, specifically minorities and women. The award is for one academic year of tuition plus stipends of $10,000 a year. Applicants must be students with an interest in the electronics industry who are pursuing a degree in computer science, engineering, materials science, chemistry, physics, or mathematics. The deadline is February 1.

*Contact:* IBM
T.J. Watson Research Center
P.O. Box 218
Yorktown Heights, NY 10598
914-945-3000

### The Metropolitan Museum of Art

This is an honorarium for interns; its monthly value is $1,250. Applicants must be African-American or Hispanic American graduate students in art history or related fields. The deadline is February 17.

*Contact:* The Metropolitan Museum of Art
Internships for African American and
Hispanic American Students
Office of Academic Programs
Fifth Avenue at 82nd Street
New York, NY 10028
212-535-7710

### Minority Access Program (MAP)

Begun in the summer of 1989, MAP is designed to encourage minority students to enter the fields of public service and international affairs at both the national and state levels. Awards include a one-year fellowship that provides tuition and a $7,000 stipend; the institution also receives $6,000 toward the cost of tuition from the foundation. Participating students are required to attend a Junior Institute in the summer after their junior year in college, and they can choose among three opportunities for the summer of their senior year—an internship, a Senior Institute, or language studies.

*Contact:* Richard O. Hope, Director
Minority Access Program
Woodrow Wilson National Fellowship Foundation
Box 642, 330 Alexander Street
Princeton, NJ 08542
609-924-4666

### Music Assistance Fund

There are varying amounts for varying types of graduate music programs. Applicants must be orchestra musicians—not including pianists—from minority populations. The deadline is November 1.

*Contact:* Music Assistance Fund
New York Philharmonic Avery Fisher Hall
Broadway at 65th Street
New York, NY 10023
212-825-5000

### National Consortium for Graduate Degrees for Minorities in Engineering (GEM)

GEM was formed in 1976 to help encourage minority men and women to pursue graduate study in engineering. It was created specifically to assist Native American, African-American, Mexican-American, and Puerto Rican students in obtaining practical experience through summer internships at consortium employer work sites and to finance graduate study toward a master's or Ph.D. degree. GEM administers several fellowship programs, and forty fellowships are awarded annually in each. The fellowships are "portable," meaning that recipients can use them at any of the schools that participate in the GEM program. They are:

- M.S. Engineering Fellowship Program: GEM began its operation fifteen years ago with this master's fellowship program. Each fellow is provided with a GEM employer-sponsored summer internship and a portable fellowship tenable at one of sixty GEM universities. The fellowship consists of tuition, fees, and a $6,000 stipend per academic year.

- Ph.D. Fellowship Programs: The Ph.D. Science Fellowship and the Engineering Fellowship programs provide opportunities for minority students to obtain a Ph.D. degree in the natural sciences or in engineering through a program of paid summer research internships and financial support. Open to U.S. citizens who belong to one of the ethnic groups underrepresented in the natural sciences and engineering, GEM fellowships are awarded for a twelve-month period. Fellowships are tenable at universities participating in the GEM Science or Engineering Ph.D. Program. Awards include tuition, fees, and a $12,000 stipend. After the first year of study, GEM fellows are supported completely by their respective universities, and support may include teaching or research assistantships.

To be eligible, applicants must be a member of one of the groups listed above, a U.S. citizen, and a B.A./B.S. holder. The deadline is December 1; awards are announced by February 1.

*Contact:* The GEM Center
P.O. Box 537
Notre Dame, IN 46556
219-287-1097

### National Hispanic Scholarship Fund
The purpose of this competitive scholarship fund is to assist Hispanic Americans in completing their higher education. Awards generally range from $500 to $1,000.

Grants are available for graduate students of Mexican-American, Puerto Rican, Cuban, Caribbean, Central American, or South American heritage attending a college or university in the United States. Application forms can be obtained beginning in June.

*Contact:* National Hispanic Scholarship Fund
1400 Grant Avenue
Room 203-A
Novato, CA 94945
415-892-9971

### National Physical Science Consortium (NPSC)
The National Physical Science Consortium offers fellowships at participating NPSC institutions to women and minorities studying in the physical sciences. Awards are for tuition, fees, and a stipend for a maximum of six years. The stipend is $10,000 for the first two years, $12,500 for the second two years, and $15,000 for the final two years.

Fellows also earn money through the summer employment program with participating national laboratories and industries.

Applicants must be U.S. citizens who are women or are a member of one of the following minority groups: Hispanic American, Native American, African-American, Mexican-American, or Puerto Rican. The deadline is November 15; awards are announced in January.

*Contact:* Nan Snow, Executive Director
National Physical Sciences Consortium
c/o University of New Mexico, O'Loughlin House
University Boulevard, Box 30001, Dept. 3NPS
Las Cruces, NM 88003
505-646-6037

### Presbyterian Church (U.S.A.)

This is a grant for $1,000 to $1,500 per year for Asian American, African-American, Hispanic American, or Native American graduate students who are members of the Presbyterian Church, U.S.A., and are studying for professional church occupations. The deadline varies.

*Contact:* Office of Financial Aid for Studies
Presbyterian Church (U.S.A.)
Church Vocations Unit
100 Witherspoon Street
Louisville, KY 40202–1396
502-569-5776

## Minority Recruitment Initiatives

What follows are not awards for graduate study per se, but rather programs or publications designed to help locate minorities for graduate programs throughout the U.S. Some are aimed at students who want information on programs that are actively recruiting underrepresented students. Others, although aimed at institutions that need help reaching minority populations for places in graduate programs, may lead to other sources of aid.

### Graduate Record Examinations (GRE) Minority Graduate Student Locator Service

GRE provides a free service that matches minority students with graduate schools. The computer-based search service uses five variables: racial or ethnic background, intended graduate major, eventual degree objective, state of residence, and geographic preference for graduate study. Details and registration forms are available in the GRE Information Bulletin or the contact below.

*Contact:* GRE Locator Services
Educational Testing Service
P.O. Box 6004
Princeton, NJ 08541–6004
609-771-7670

## National Science Foundation

The National Science Foundation has a Directorate on Education and Human Resources. Its purpose is to match minority students with interested graduate programs.

*Contact:* Dr. Luther Williams
National Science Foundation
1800 G Street, NW
Washington, D.C. 20550
202-357-7557

## Project 1000

Project 1000 was created to recruit and retain Hispanic students in graduate programs. Among the services it provides is information on securing financial support for graduate study. U.S. citizens or permanent residents of Hispanic ethnic origin are eligible to apply. Project 1000 is administered at Arizona State University.

*Contact:* Gary Keller, Executive Director
Arizona State University
800-327-4893

## The White House Initiative on Historically Black Colleges and Universities

The major focus of this program is to establish relationships between historically African-American colleges and graduate programs around the country, especially those at major research institutions.

*Contact:* White House Initiative on Historically Black Colleges and Universities
7th and D Streets, SW
Washington, D.C. 20202-5120
202-708-8667

The following are organizations that can provide information on financial assistance programs for minority students:

Bureau of Indian Affairs
    Central Office
    Bureau of Higher Education Staff
    P.O. Box 1788
    Albuquerque, NM 87103
    505-766-3160

Indian Health Service
    Parklawn Building, Room 6–12
    5600 Fishers Lane
    Rockville, MD 20857
    301-443-1083

National Hispanic Scholarship Fund
    P.O. Box 748
    San Francisco, CA 94101
    415-892-9971

National Research Council
    2101 Constitution Avenue, NW
    Washington, D.C. 20418
    202-334-2872

United Negro College Fund
    500 East 62nd Street
    New York, NY 10021
    212-326-1100

See Appendix B for publications that provide information on both public and private financial assistance programs for minority students.

# WOMEN

Like minority groups, women have traditionally been underrepresented in many graduate areas. Physical science and engineering, in particular, have far fewer women than men in their graduate programs. The table on page 157, provided by the Council of Graduate Schools, shows the distribution of female and male graduate students in these fields as well as seven other fields of study.

Because of such unequal distribution, organizations like the National Physical Science Consortium have chosen to give funding

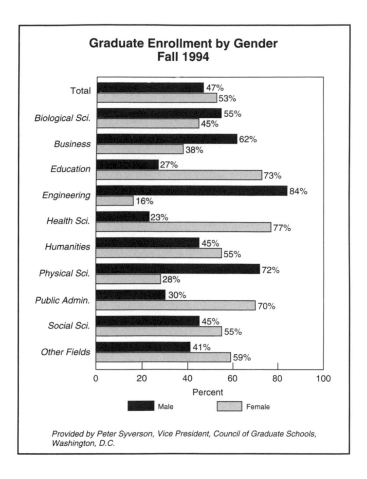

Graduate Enrollment by Gender
Fall 1994

Provided by Peter Syverson, Vice President, Council of Graduate Schools, Washington, D.C.

priority to women as well as to minority students. For information on its programs, see its listing in the section "Privately Sponsored Grants for Minorities" earlier in this chapter. What follows are other organizations that give financial aid specifically to women.

## American Association of University Women Educational Foundation

The American Association of University Women awards several different grants and fellowships each year to women who wish to further their postgraduate education. Last year, the AAUW Educational Foundation awarded more than $2.5 million in fellowships and grants to 269 women for community action projects, individual research, and formal academic pursuits. Award amounts range between $500 and $25,000.

*Contact:* AAUW Educational Foundation
2201 N. Dodge Street
Iowa City, IA 52243-4030
319-337-1716

## Business and Professional Women's Foundations

This is a grant/scholarship award for any field of graduate study. Funds may be used for living expenses, tuition and fees, travel costs, or support for spouse/dependents. The number available ranges from thirty to fifty. In the most recent award period there were ninety applicants. Awards range from $500 to $1,000.

Four different awards are made annually:

- The BPW Career Advancement Scholarship is a $500 to $1,000 award for women at least 25 years old.

- The Clairol Scholarship is a $500 to $1,000 award for women at least 25 years old.

- The Avon Products Foundation Scholarship is a $500 to $1,000 award to women heads of households supporting one or more dependents and pursuing education leading to a sales career.

- The St. Paul Foundation Scholarship is a $500 to $1,000 award for black women over 25.

Note: Applicants for all programs must be graduating within twenty-four months of receiving the award. Education must lead to entry or reentry into the workforce or improve changes for advancement. Financial need must be demonstrated. For more information or an application, send a self-addressed stamped envelope to the contact below.

*Contact:* Liana Sayer
Associate Education and Training
BPW Career Advancement Scholarship
BPW Foundation
2012 Massachusetts Avenue, NW
Washington, D.C. 20036
202-296-9118

## Canadian Federation of University Women

This is a fellowship award for any field of graduate study. Funds may be used for any purpose desired by the recipient. One award of $1,000 is available. Applicants must be B.A./B.S. holders, women, and Canadian citizens. Recipients are selected on the basis of academic achievement.

Application forms are available August 1 from the contact and are due December 1; recipients are announced May 31.

*Contact:* Bourse Georgette Lemoyne
Canadian Federation of University Women
55 Parkdale Avenue
Ottawa, ON K1Y 1E5
Canada
613-722-8732

### Gilette Hayden Memorial Foundation of the American Association of Women Dentists

The Gilette Hayden Memorial Foundation Loan is a low-interest loan award of up to $2,000 available for study in the field of dentistry. Funds may be used for school or specialty training. Applicants must be in the second year of dental school. Recipients are selected on the basis of academic achievement, financial need, and reasons for and amounts of previous indebtedness. Application forms are available year-round from contact and are due August 1. Recipients are announced on or before October 1.

*Contact:* Dr. Goldana Cramer
Gilette Hayden Memorial Foundation Loans
American Association of Women Dentists
95 West Broadway
Salem, NJ 08079
609-935-0467

### Kappa Gamma Fraternity

This is a grant/scholarship award for any field of graduate study. Funds may be used for tuition and fees. There are twenty to thirty $750 awards offered once a year. Applicants must be B.A./B.S. holders. Recipients are selected on the basis of financial need. They must be women, U.S. citizens, and members of Kappa Gamma Fraternity. Application forms are available year-round from the contact and are accepted continuously.

*Contact:* Circle Key Grants of Rose McGill
Kappa Gamma Fraternity
P.O. Box 2079
Columbus, OH 43216
614-228-6515

## National Collegiate Athletic Association

The NCAA Women's Sports Administration Internship Program awards three to five internship/trainee positions each year to be used in the field of sports administration for any field of study beyond the bachelor's. Funds may be used for any use desired by the recipient. The award value ranges up to $12,000.

Recipients are selected on the basis of academic achievement and quality of proposed research. Applicants planning employment in sports administration are preferred. Application forms are available October 1 from the contact and are due March 15.

*Contact:* Stanley D. Johnson
Director of Professional Development
NCAA Women's Sports Administration
National Collegiate Athletic Association
Women's Enhancement Program
P.O. Box 1906
Mission, KS 66201
913-384-3220

## Society of Women Engineers

This is a grant/scholarship to be used for graduate-level engineering study. Funds may be used for research costs, living expenses, tuition and fees, travel costs, secretarial/research assistance, or support for spouse/dependents. Approximately thirty-eight are awarded annually and range in value from $500 to $2,500.

Applicants must be women graduate students. Recipients are selected on the basis of academic achievement. Applications are available March 1 from the contact and are due July 1. Recipients are announced September 15.

*Contact:* Society of Women Engineering Scholarship
345 East 47th Street
New York, NY 10017
212-705-7855

## Wellesley College—M.A. Cartland Shackford Medical Fellowship

This is a fellowship award for general practice medicine. Funds may be used for tuition and fees. The award ranges in value up to $3,500.

Applicants must be women medical students. Recipients are selected on the basis of academic achievement and financial need. Applications are due December 1.

*Contact:* Secretary to the Committee on Graduate Fellowships
M.A. Cartland Shackford Medical Fellowship
Wellesley College
Office of Financial Aid, Box GR
Wellesley, MA 02181
617-283-2360

## Wellesley College

This is a fellowship award for any field of graduate study. Funds may be used for tuition and fees. The award is valued at $4,000. Applicants must be B.A./B.S. holders, women, unmarried, and up to 26 years old. Recipients are selected on the basis of academic achievement and financial need. Applicants apply though their institutions; applications are available through the contact and are due December 1.

*Contact:* Secretary to the Committee on Graduate Fellowships
Alice Freeman Palmer Fellowship
Wellesley College
Office of Financial Aid, Box GR
Wellesley, MA 02181
617-283-2360

## Women's Research and Education Institute—Congressional Fellowships on Women and Public Policy

This is a fellowship award applicable to most humanities and social sciences, biology and biomedical sciences, engineering and applied sciences, biomedical engineering, technology management and policy, business administration and management, health services management and hospital administration, education, allied health professions, medicine, nursing, nutrition, public and community health, and law. Funds may be used for living expenses, tuition, and fees. The award value is $11,000.

Applicants must be master's or doctoral candidates who are women. Recipients are selected on the basis of academic achievement, financial need, quality of proposed research, political/civic activity, and interest in women's policy issues. Application forms are available December 1 from the contact and are due in mid-February. Recipients are announced May 1.

*Contact:*  Alison Dineen
           Fellowship Program Director
           Congressional Fellowships on Women and Public Policy
           Women's Research and Education Institute
           1700 18th Street, NW #400
           Washington, D.C. 20009
           202-328-7070

**Zonta International Foundation**

The Zonta Amelia Earhart Fellowship is a grant/fellowship for aerospace-related science and engineering study at the master's or doctoral level. Funds may be used for tuition and fees or books. There are forty awards made annually for $6,000.

Applicants must be B.A./B.S. holders who are women planning employment in aeronautics or teaching and/or research. Recipients are selected on the basis of academic achievement (4.0 GPA preferred). Applications must be postmarked by November 1 and received at Zonta International Headquarters by November 7. Recipients are announced May 15.

*Contact:*  Rickie M. Jacobs
           Foundation Manager
           Zonta Amelia Earhart Fellowship Awards
           Zonta International Foundation
           557 West Randolph Street
           Chicago, IL 60606–2284
           312-930-5848

See Appendix C for publications that provide information on financial assistance programs—both public and private—for women.

# VETERANS

Veterans Educational Benefits may be used at the graduate level. If you are a veteran and contributed to one of the programs, you are entitled to education benefits provided that you have completed at least one year of active service in the U.S. Armed Forces; if you were discharged under honorable conditions for medical reasons, you may be eligible even if you spent less than one year in active service. You do not have to demonstrate financial need to be eligible for these programs; they are a benefit to which you are entitled automatically. The amount of educational benefits a veteran receives depends on the length of military service, the number of dependents and the number of semester credits carried. Some states offer special programs for veterans.

### Montgomery G.I. Bill

This is most like the old G.I. Bill. It is for veterans who entered the service after July 1, 1985, served two years of continuous active duty, accepted a $100-a-month reduction in their military pay for the first twelve months of service, and received an honorable discharge. The monthly rate depends on the veteran's length of active duty service or service in the Selective Reserve or the National Guard. The benefits entitlement period is thirty-six months of full-time enrollment or the part-time equivalent in a graduate program.

You can access information on the Montgomery G.I. Bill via the Internet at the following address:

http://www.va.gov/pub/benman95/301SAB2.HTM#educ

### Post-Vietnam Era Veterans' Educational Assistance Program (VEAP)

This is a program for veterans who entered active duty between January 1, 1977, and July 1, 1985, and who enrolled in the VEAP program before April 1, 1987. A veteran must have served a continuous period of at least 181 days and have received an honorable discharge to be eligible. There is a voluntary matching program available in which enlistees on active duty contributed $25 to $100 per month up to a maximum of $2,700; the government then matches this contribution two to one. Recipients receive monthly payments for up to thirty-six months. The amount received depends on the number of months enrolled in graduate school, enrollment status, and the total amount in the veteran's fund.

You can access information on VEAP via the Internet at the following address: http://www.va.gov/pub/benman95/301SAB2.HTM#veap

### Survivors' and Dependents' Educational Assistance Fund (DEAP)

In addition to educational benefits for veterans, there is also a program for the child or spouse of a veteran who has died or is permanently and totally disabled as a result of active service: the Survivors' and Dependents' Educational Assistance Fund (DEAP). There is a limit of forty-five months of eligibility, and you must be between the ages of 18 and 26 to qualify. The monthly payment is fixed at a rate determined by the government. The spouses' eligibility extends up to ten years.

Further information can be obtained from the Office of Veterans Affairs at your school and from a booklet, "Federal Benefits for Veteran and Dependents," published by the Veterans Affairs Department, 810 Vermont Ave., Washington, D.C. 20420, 202-233-4000. You can also access this booklet online at the following address: http://www.va.gov/pub/benman95/5SURVIVO.HTM#educate

# ppendices

## Appendix A: General Information on Graduate Financial Support

### Directories and Books

*American Legion Educational Program. Need a Lift? To Educational Opportunities, Careers, Loans, Scholarships, Employment.* 44th ed. Indianapolis: American Legion, 1995.

Bowker, R.R. *Annual Register of Grant Support 1996.* New Providence, N.J.: Reed Reference Publishing Company, 1996.

Cassidy, Daniel J. *The Graduate Scholarship Book: The Complete Guide to Scholarships, Fellowships, Grants and Loans for Graduate and Professional Study.* 2nd ed. Englewood Cliffs: Prentice Hall, 1990.

*Catalogue of Federal Domestic Assistance.* Washington, D.C.: U.S. Office of Management and Budget, 1987.

*Corporate Foundation Profiles.* 8th ed. New York: The Foundation Center, 1994.

*Directory of Biomedical and Health Care Grants 1996.* 10th ed. Phoenix: Oryx Press, 1995.

*Directory of Grants in the Humanities 1995-1996.* 9th ed. Phoenix: Oryx Press, 1995.

*Directory of Research Grants 1996.* Vol. 2276. Phoenix: Oryx Press, 1995.

*Fellowships and Grants for Training and Research, 1992-1993.* New York: Social Science Research Council, 1992.

*Foundation Grants to Individuals.* 9th ed. New York: The Foundation Center, 1993.

*Graduate Guide to Grants 1994-1995.* Cambridge, MA: Harvard University, Graduate School of Arts and Sciences, 1995.

*Grants and Fellowship Opportunities of Interest to Philosophers, 1988-1989.* Newark, DE: American Philosophical Association, 1988.

*Grants, Fellowships, and Prizes of Interest to Historians, 1994-1995.* Washington, D.C.: American Historical Association, 1995.

*Guide to Grants and Fellowships in Linguistics, 1991.* Washington, D.C.: Linguistic Society of America, 1991.

Koek, Karin E., and Susan Boyles Martin, eds. *Encyclopedia of Associations—1993.* 27th ed. 3 vols. Detroit: Gale Research Company, 1993.

McWade, Patricia. *Financial Aid for Graduate and Professional Education.* 10th ed. Princeton, N.J.: Peterson's Guides, 1995.

Olsen, Stan, ed. *Foundation Directory.* 20th ed. New York: Foundation Center, 1994.

Schlachter, Gail Ann. *How to Find Out About Financial Aid 1995-1997 Edition.* Los Angeles: Reference Service Press, 1995.

*Scholarships, Fellowships, and Loans, 1991-1995.* 10th ed. Detroit: Gale Research Inc., 1994.

*A Selected List of Fellowship Opportunities and Aids to Advanced Education.* Washington, D.C.: The Publications Office, National Science Foundation, 1988.

Williams, Lisa, ed. *The Grants Register 1995-97.* 14th ed. New York: St. Martin's Press, 1994 .

**Periodicals**

*ARIS Funding Messenger—The Student Report.* San Francisco: Academic Research Information System, Inc. Published five times each year; includes details on both undergraduate and graduate funds and how to apply for them.

# Appendix B: Information on Financial Support for Minorities

*Financial Aid for Minorities: Awards Open to Students With Any Major.* Garrett Park, Md.: Garrett Park Press, 1994.

*Financial Aid for Minorities in Business and Law.* Garrett Park, Md.: Garrett Park Press, 1994.

*Financial Aid for Minorities in Education.* Garrett Park, Md.: Garrett Park Press, 1993.

*Financial Aid for Minorities in Engineering and Science.* Garrett Park, Md.: Garrett Park Press, 1992.

*Financial Aid for Minorities in Health Fields.* Garrett Park, Md.: Garrett Park Press, 1995.

*Financial Aid for Minorities in Journalism and Mass Communications* Garrett Park, Md.: Garrett Park Press, 1994.

Schlachter, Gail Ann, and R. David Weber. *Directory of Financial Aid for Minorities, 1995-1997.* Los Angeles, Calif.: Reference Service Press, 1995.

Stanford University, Office of Graduate Studies, Office of Recruitment and Retention. "Sources of Funding for Minority Graduate Students." Stanford, Calif.: 1990.

Verba, Cynthia. Harvard University Graduate School of Arts and Science, "Minorities in Academe: A Guide to Becoming a Scholar." Cambridge, MASS.: 1989.

## Appendix C: Information on Financial Support for Women

*Grants At A Glance: A Directory of Funding and Financial Aid Resources for Women in Science, 1992.* 2nd ed. Washington, D.C.: Association for Women in Science.

Rubin, Mary. *How to Get Money for Research.* 1st ed. Old Westbury, N.Y.: Feminist Press, 1987.

Schlachter, Gail Ann. *Directory of Financial Aid for Women, 1995-1997.* Redwood City, Calif.: Reference Service Press, 1995.

## Appendix D: Information on Financial Support for Study Abroad

*Awards for Postgraduate Study in Australia.* Victoria, Australia: Graduate Career Council of Australia, 1984.

*Basic Facts on Foreign Study.* New York: Institute for International Education, 1986.

*Commonwealth Universities Yearbook 1994.* 70th ed. 4 Vols. London: Association of Commonwealth Universities, 1994.

*Fellowships, Scholarships, and Related Opportunities in International Education.* Knoxville, Tenn.: The Center, 1989.

Franz, Del, Hernandez, and Lazaro, eds. *Work, Study, Travel Abroad, 1994-1995.* 12th ed. New York: St. Martin's Press, 1994.

"Fulbright Grants and Other Grants for Graduate Study Abroad." New York: Institute of International Education, 1993-1994.

*Higher Education in the United Kingdom.* Harlow, England: Longman UK Ltd., 1991.

Hoopes, David S. *Global Guide to International Education.* 2nd ed. Detroit: Gale Research, 1991.

Institute of International Education, eds. *Financial Resources for International Study.* Princeton, N.J.: Peterson's Guides, 1989.

List of Organizations Involved in Exchange Programs with the Soviet
Union and Eastern Europe. Washington, D.C.: U.S. Government
Printing Office, 1986.
"Transitions Abroad: Guide to International Study, Work, and Travel,"
Amherst, Mass.: C.A. Hubbs 1985.

## Appendix E: Information on Financial Support of International Students

Bones, Gregory A. *The International Student's Guide to the American
University*. Lincolnwood, Ill, National Textbook Company, 1993.
Includes a chapter on financial aid.
*Directory of Research Grants 1996*. Phoenix: Oryx Press, 1995.
*Funding for U.S. Study: A Guide for Foreign Nationals*. New York:
Institute of International Education, 1990.
*Grants for Graduate Study, 1994*. 4th ed. Princeton, N.J.: Peterson's
Guides, 1994.
*Scholarships for International Students, A Complete Guide to
Colleges and Universities in the U.S.* Alexandria, Va.: Octameron
Press, 1988.
*A Selected List of Fellowships and Aid to Advanced Education for U.S.
Citizens and Foreign Nationals.* National Science Foundation,
Washington, D.C., 1994
Williams, Lisa, ed. *The Grants Register 1995-1997*. 14th ed. New
York: St. Martin's Press, 1994.
Wicksemasinge, W. *Scholarships and Grants for Study or Research in
the USA*. Houston, Tex, American Collegiate Service, 1987.

## Appendix F: Glossary of Acronyms

ABA—American Bar Association
AALS—Association of American Law Schools
AAMC—Association of American Medical Schools
ABD—All but dissertation
ALP—Alternative Loan Program, the private loan part of the
MedLoans program
BEOG—Basic Educational Opportunity Grant, now called Pell
Grant, not available to graduate students
BIA—Bureau of Indian Affairs
DOE—Department of Energy, not to be confused with the
Department of Education (ED)
USDE—United States Department of Education

FAFSA—Free Application for Federal Student Aid
FAO—Financial Aid Office or Financial Aid Officer
FAT—Financial Aid Transcript
FICA—Federal Insurance Corporation of America (Social Security tax)
FLAS—Foreign Language and Area Studies Fellowship
FM—Federal Methodology, the federally approved need analysis system
FSEOG—Federal Supplemental Educational Opportunity Grant, a federal grant for undergraduates only
FWS—Federal Work-Study Program
FY—Fiscal Year; for the U.S. government the fiscal year runs from October 1 through September 30
GEM—Graduate Education for Minorities
GMAC—Graduate Management Admissions Council
GRA—Graduate research assistant, sometimes called an RA
GRE—Graduate Record Examinations
GSL—Guaranteed Student Loan, now called Stafford Loan, a federally subsidized loan
GTA—Graduate teaching assistant, sometimes called teaching assistant, TA, or teaching fellow, TF
HACU—Hispanic Association of Colleges and Universities
HBCU—Historically Black Colleges and Universities
HEA—Higher Education Act
HEAL—Health Education Assistance Loan
IIE—Institute of International Education
IM—Institutional Methodology, a need analyses system used by some graduate schools to award their own funds
IREX—International Research and Exchange Board
LAL—Law Access Loan, the private loan offered by The Access Group
NAFSA—Association of International Educators, formerly the National Association for Foreign Student Affairs
NAS—National Academy of Sciences
NASA—National Aeronautics and Space Administration
NASFAA—National Association of Student Financial Aid Administrators
NDSL—National Direct Student Loan, now called Perkins Loan, a federal, low-interest loan
NELLIE MAE—New England Loan Marketing Association, a regional secondary loan market

NIH—National Institutes of Health

NIJ—National Institute of Justice

NIMH—National Institute of Mental Health

NPRM—Notice of Proposed Rule Making

NPSAS—National Postsecondary Student Aid Study, produced by the U.S. Department of Education, Office of Educational Research and Improvement

NRC—National Research Council

NRSA—National Research Service Award

NSF—National Science Foundation

NUCEA—National University Continuing Education Association

ONR—Office of Naval Research

PCL—Primary Care Loan

PHS—Public Health Service

PRH—Patricia Roberts Harris Fellowship Programs

RA—Research assistant, sometimes called graduate research assistant, GRA

SALLIE MAE—Student Loan Marketing Association, a national secondary loan market

SSCR—Social Science Research Council

TA—Teaching assistant, sometimes called teaching fellow, TF, or graduate teaching assistant, GTA

TERI—The Education Resources Institute, a private loan program

TF—Teaching fellow, sometimes called teaching assistant, TA, or graduate teaching assistant, GTA

USAF—United Student Aid Fund, a national loan guarantee agency

USIA—United States Information Agency

VA—Veterans Administration

# Appendix G: State Student Scholarship Agencies

**Alabama**
Alabama Commission on Higher
  Education
3465 Norman Bridge Road, Suite 230
Montgomery, AL 36105-2310
(205) 281-1921

**Alaska**
Alaska Commission on Postsecondary
  Education
3030 Vintage Boulevard
Juneau, AK 99801-7109
(907) 465-2962

**Arizona**
Commission for Postsecondary Education
2020 North Central Avenue, Suite 275
Phoenix, AZ 85004
(602) 229-2593

**Arkansas**
Department of Higher Education
114 East Capitol
Little Rock, AR 72201-3818
(501) 324-9300

**California**
California Student Aid Commission
PO Box 510845
Sacramento, CA 94245-0845
(916) 445-0880

**Colorado**
Colorado Commission on Higher
  Education
1300 Broadway, 2nd Floor
Denver, CO 80203
(303) 866-2723

**Connecticut**
Connecticut Department of Higher
  Education
61 Woodland Street
Hartford, CT 06105-2391
(203) 566-2618

**Delaware**
Delaware Higher Education Commission
Carvel State Office Building, 4th Floor
820 North French Street
Wilmington, DE 19801
(302) 577-3240

**District of Columbia**
D.C. Office of Postsecondary Education
Research and Assistance
D.C. Department of Human Services
2100 Martin Luther King Jr. Avenue, SE
Suite 401
Washington, D.C. 20020
(202) 727-3685

**Florida**
Office of Student Financial Assistance
1344 Florida Education Center
Tallahassee, FL 32399-0400
(904) 488-1034

**Georgia**
Georgia Student Finance Commission
State Loans and Grants Division
2082 East Exchange Place, Suite 245
Tucker, GA 30084
(404) 414-3084

**Hawaii**
Hawaii State Postsecondary Education
  Commission
2444 Dole Street Room 209
Honolulu, HI 96822-2394
(808) 956-8207

**Idaho**
Office of State Board of Education
P.O. Box 83720
Boise, ID 83720-0037
(208) 334-2270

## Illinois
Illinois Student Assistance Commission
1755 Lake Cook Road
Deerfield, IL 60015-5209
(708) 948-8500

## Indiana
State Student Assistance
Commission of Indiana
150 West Market Street, Suite 500
Indianapolis, IN 46204-2811
(317) 232-2350

## Iowa
Iowa College Student Aid Commission
914 Grand Avenue, Suite 201
Des Moines, IA 50309-2824
(515) 242-5067

## Kansas
Kansas Board of Regents
700 SW Harrison, Suite 1410
Topeka, KS 66003-3760
(913) 296-3517

## Kentucky
Kentucky Higher Education Assistant
   Authority
1050 U.S. 127 South
Suite 102
Frankfort, KY 40601-4323
(800) 928-8926

## Louisiana
Louisiana Student Financial Assistance
   Commission
Office of Student Financial Assistance
P.O. Box 91202
Baton Rouge, LA 70821-9202
(504) 922-1150

## Maine
Finance Authority of Maine
State House Station 119
One Weston Court
Augusta, ME 04333
(207) 287-2183

## Maryland
Maryland Higher Education Commission
Maryland State Scholarship Administra-
tion
Jeffrey Building, Suite 219
16 Francis Street
Annapolis, MD 21401-1781
(410) 974-5370

## Massachusetts
Massachusetts Higher Education
   Coordinating Counsel
330 Stuart Street
Boston, MA 02116
(617) 727-4860

## Michigan
Michigan Department of Education
Scholar and Tuition Grant Program
P.O. Box 30008
Lansing, MI 48909
(517) 373-3394

## Minnesota
Minnesota Higher Education Coordinating
   Board
Capitol Square Building, Suite 400
550 Cedar Street
Saint Paul, MN 55101
(612) 298-3974

## Mississippi
Mississippi Postsecondary Education
Financial Assistance Board
3825 Ridgewood Road
Jackson, MS 39211-6453
(601) 982-6663

## Missouri
Missouri Coordinating Board for Higher
   Education
Missouri Student Grant Program
3515 Amazonas Drive
Jefferson City, MO 65109-5717
(314) 751-2361

**Montana**
Montana University Systems
2500 Broadway
Helena, MT 59620-3103
(406) 444-0351

**Nebraska**
Nebraska Coordinating Commission for
  Postsecondary Education
P.O. Box 95005
Lincoln, NE 68509-5005
(402) 471-2847

**Nevada**
Nevada Department of Education
Administrative and Fiscal Services
400 West King Street, Capitol Complex
Carson City, NV 89710
(702) 687-5915

**New Hampshire**
New Hampshire Postsecondary Education
  Commission
2 Industrial Park Drive
Concord, NH 03301-8512
(603) 271-2555

**New Jersey**
Office of Student Assistance
4 Quakerbridge Plaza, C.N. 540
Trenton, NJ 08625
(609) 588-3268

**New Mexico**
Commission on Higher Education
1068 Cerrilos Road
Santa Fe, NM 87501-4295
(505) 827-7383

**New York**
New York State Higher Education
  Services Corporation
One Commerce Plaza
Albany, NY 12255
(518) 473-0431

**North Carolina**
North Carolina State Education
  Assistance Authority
P.O. Box 2688
Chapel Hill, NC 27515-2688
(919) 549-8614

**North Dakota**
North Dakota Student Financial
  Assistance Program
600 East Boulevard Avenue
Bismarck, ND 58505-0230
(701) 224-4114

**Ohio**
Ohio Student Aid Commission
309 South Fourth Street
PO Box 182452
Columbus, OH 43218-2452
(614) 752-9488

**Oklahoma**
Oklahoma State Regents for Higher
  Education
500 Education Building
State Capital Complex
Oklahoma City, OK 73105-4503
(405) 552-4356

**Oregon**
Oregon State Scholarship Commission
1500 Valley River Drive, Suite 100
Eugene, OR 97401
(503) 687-7385

**Pennsylvania**
Pennsylvania Higher Education
  Assistance Agency
1200 North Seventh Street
Harrisburg, PA 17102-1444
(717) 257-2800

**Rhode Island**
Rhode Island Higher Education
  Assistance Authority
560 Jefferson Boulevard
Warwick, RI 02886
(401) 736-1100

## South Carolina

South Carolina Higher Education Tuition
  Grants Commission
1310 Lady Street, Suite 811
Box 12159
Columbia, SC 29211
(803) 734-1200

## South Dakota

South Dakota Department of Education
  and Cultural Affairs
Office of the Secretary
700 Governors Drive
Pierre, SD 57501-2291
(605) 773-3134

## Tennessee

Tennessee Student Assistance Corporation
Parkway Towers, Suite 1950
404 James Robertson Parkway
Nashville, TN 37243-0820
(615) 741-1346

## Texas

Texas Higher Education Coordinating
  Board
Capitol Station
P.O. Box 12788
Austin, TX 78711
(512) 483-6331

## Utah

Utah System of Higher Education
355 West North Temple
3 Triad Center, Suite 550
Salt Lake City, UT 84180-1205
(801) 321-7205

## Vermont

Vermont Student Assistance Corporation
Champlain Mill
P.O. Box 2000
Winooski, VT 05404-2601
(802) 655-9602

## Virginia

State Council of Higher Education for
  Virginia
James Monroe Building
101 North 14th Street
Richmond, VA 23219
(804) 225-2623

## Washington

Washington State Higher Education
  Coordinating Board
917 Lakeridge Way
P.O. Box 43430
Olympia, WA 98504-3430
(206) 753-3521

## West Virginia

Central Office, State College and
  University Systems of West Virginia
1018 Kanawha Boulevard East
Suite 700
Charleston, WV 25301-2827
(304) 347-1266

## Wisconsin

Wisconsin Higher Education Aids Board
P.O. Box 7885
Madison, WI 53707-7885
(608) 266-1660

## Wyoming

Wyoming Community College
  Commission
Herschler Building 1W
122 West 25th Street
Cheyenne, WY 82002
(307) 777-7763

# Appendix H—State Student Loan Guarantee Agencies

**Alabama**
Alabama Commission on Higher
  Education
1 Court Square, Suite 221
Montgomery, AL 36104–3584
(205) 269–2700

**Alaska**
Alaska Commission on Postsecondary
  Education
Alaska Student Loan Corporation
P.O. Box 110505
Juneau, AK 99811-0505
(907) 465-2854

**Arizona**
Arizona Educational Loan Program
United Student Aid Funds, Inc.
P.O. Box 3028
Chandler, AZ 85244-3028
(606) 815-9988

**Arkansas**
Student Loan Guarantee Foundation of
  Arkansas
291 South Victory Street
Little Rock, AR 72201-1884
(501) 372–1491
(800) 622-3446

**California**
California Student Aid Commission
P.O. Box 510845
Sacramento, CA 94245–0845
(916) 445-0880
(800) 367-1589 (to make payment arrangements)
(916) 322-9277 (billing problems)

**Colorado**
Colorado Guaranteed Student Loan
  Program
999 18th Street, Suite 425
Denver, CO 80202-2440
(303) 294-5069 (status check)
(303) 294-5050 (main number)
(800) 289-7378

**Connecticut**
Connecticut Student Loan Foundation
525 Brook Street
P.O. Box 1009
Rocky Hill, CT 06067
(203) 257-4001
(800) 237-9721 (within Connecticut)
(800) 345-6055 (outside Connecticut)

**Delaware**
Delaware Higher Education Loan
  Program
Carvel State Office Building
820 N. French Street, 4th Floor
Wilmington, DE 19801
(302) 577–6055

**District of Columbia**
American Student Assistance
330 Stuart Street
Boston, MA 02116-5292
(617) 426-9796
(800) 999-9080

**Florida**
Florida Department of Education
Office of Student Financial Assistance
325 West Gaines Street
1344 Florida Education Center
Tallahassee, FL 32395–0400
(904) 488-4095
(800) 622-1041 (within Florida)

**Georgia**
Georgia Student Finance Commission
2082 East Exchange Place, Suite 200
Tucker, GA 30084
(404) 493-5402
(800) 776-6878

**Hawaii**
Hawaii Education Loan Program
P.O. Box 22187
Honolulu, HI 96823–0187
(808) 536–3731

**Idaho**
Student Loan Fund of Idaho, Inc.
P.O. Box 730
Fruitland, ID 83619
(208) 452–4058
(800) 528-9447 (within Idaho)

**Illinois**
Illinois Student Assistance Commission
1755 Lake Cook Road
Deerfield, IL 60015
(708) 948–8500

**Indiana**
State Student Assistance Commission of
  Indiana
Loan Division
150 West Market, 5th Floor
Indianapolis, IN 46204-1032
(317) 232-2366

**Iowa**
Iowa College Student Aid Commission
Suite 201 Jewett Building
914 Grand Avenue
Des Moines, IA 50309-2824
(515) 281–4890
(800) 383-4222

**Kansas**
United Student Aid Funds, Inc.
USA Group
11100 USA Parkway
Fishers, IN 46038
(800) 824-7044
or
USA Group
P.O. Box 6180
Indianapolis, IN 46026-6180

**Kentucky**
Kentucky Education Assistance Authority
1050 U.S. 127 South
Suite 120
Frankfort, KY 40601
(502) 564–7990
(800) 928-8926

**Louisiana**
Louisiana Office of Student Financial
  Assistance
P.O. Box 91202
Baton Rouge, LA 70821-9202
(504) 922–1011
(800) 259-5626

**Maine**
Finance Authority of Maine
1 Weston Court
State House Station 119
Augusta, ME 04333
(207) 289–2183
(800) 228-3734 (within Maine)

**Maryland**
USAF
(410) 333–6555

**Massachusetts**
American Student Assistance
330 Stuart Street
Boston, MA 02116
(617) 426–9434
(800) 999-9080

**Michigan**
Michigan Guarantee Agency
P.O. Box 30047
Lansing, MI 48909
(517) 373–0760
(800) 642-5626

**Minnesota**
Northstar Guarantee, Inc.
444 Cedar Street, Suite 1910
St. Paul, MN 55101-2133
or
P.O. Box 64102
St. Paul, MN 55164-0102
(612) 290-8795
(800) 366-0032

**176**

**Mississippi**
Mississippi Guarantee Student Loan
 Agency
3825 Ridgewood Road
Jackson, MS 39211
(601) 982–6663
(800) 228-3144 (within Mississippi)
(800) 327-2980 (outside Mississippi)

**Missouri**
Coordinating Board for Higher Education
101 Adams
Jefferson City, MO 65101
(314) 751–3940
(800) 473-6757 (within Missouri)

**Montana**
Montana Guaranteed Student Loan
 Program
2500 Broadway
Helena, MT 59620-3103
(406) 444–6594
(800) 537-7508

**Nebraska**
Nebraska Student Loan Program
P.O. Box 82507
Lincoln, NE 68501-2505
(402) 475–8686

**Nevada**
United Student Aid Funds, Inc.
USA Group
11100 USA Parkway
Fishers, IN 46038

**New Hampshire**
New Hampshire Higher Education
 Assistance Foundation
P.O. Box 877
Concord, NH 03302
(603) 225–6612
(800) 525-2577

**New Jersey**
New Jersey Higher Education Assistance
 Authority
Guaranteed Student Loan Program
4 Quakerbridge Plaza CN 543
Trenton, NJ 08625
(609) 588–3200
(800) 356-5562

**New Mexico**
New Mexico Student Loan Guarantee
 Corporation
P.O. Box 27020
Albuquerque, NM 87125–7020
(505) 345–8821
(800) 279-3070

**New York**
New York State Higher Education
 Services Corporation
99 Washington Ave.
Albany, NY 12255
(518) 474-5592
(800) 642-6234

**North Carolina**
North Carolina State Education
 Assistance Authority
P.O. Box 2688
Chapel Hill, NC 27515
(919) 549–8614

**North Dakota**
North Dakota Guaranteed Student Loan
 Program
PO Box 5509
Bismarck, ND 58502–5509
(701) 224–5600

**Ohio**
Ohio Student Aid Commission
309 South 4th Street
Columbus, OH 43215
(614) 466–3091
(800) 837-6752

**Oklahoma**
Oklahoma State Regents for Higher
  Education
P.O. Box 3000
Oklahoma City, OK 73105-3000
(405) 524–9100
(800) 247-0420

**Oregon**
Oregon State Scholarship Commission
1500 Valley River Drive, Suite 100
Eugene, OR 97401
(800) 452–8807 (within Oregon)
(503) 686–3200 (in state)

**Pennsylvania**
Pennsylvania Higher Education
  Assistance Agency
660 Boas Street
Harrisburg, PA 17102
(800) 692–7392
(717) 257-2500

**Rhode Island**
Rhode Island Higher Education
  Assistance Authority
560 Jefferson Boulevard
Warwick, RI 02886
(401) 277-2050
(800) 922-9855 (outside Rhode Island)

**South Carolina**
South Carolina Student Loan Corporation
16 Berry Hill Road
Interstate Center Suite 210
P.O. Box 21487
Columbia, SC 29210
(803) 798–0916

**South Dakota**
Education Assistance Corporation
115 First Ave., SW
Aberdeen, SD 57401
(605) 225–6423

**Tennessee**
Tennessee Student Assistance Corporation
404 James Robertson Parkway, Suite 1950
Parkway Towers
Nashville, TN 37243–0820
(615) 741–1346
(800) 342-1663 (within Tennessee)

**Texas**
Texas Guaranteed Student Loan
  Corporation
P.O. Box 15996
Austin, TX 78761
(512) 835–1900
(800) 252-9753

**Utah**
Utah Higher Education Assistance
  Authority
P.O. Box 45202
Salt Lake City, UT 84145-0202
(801) 538-5240

**Vermont**
Vermont Student Assistance Corporation
Champlain Mill
P.O. Box 2000
Winooskie, VT 05404–2000
(802) 655–9602
(800) 642-3177 (within Vermont)

**Virginia**
Virginia State Education Assistance
  Authority
411 East Franklin Street, Suite 300
Richmond, VA 23219
(804) 775-4000

**Washington**
Northwest Education Loan Association
500 Colman Building
811 First Avenue
Seattle, WA 98104
(206) 461-5300

**West Virginia**
Higher Education Assistance Foundation
Higher Education Loan Program of West
　Virginia
P.O. Box 591
Charleston, WV 25322
(304) 345–7211
(800) 427-3692

**Wisconsin**
Great Lakes Higher Education
　Corporation
2401 International Lane
Madison, WI 53704
(608) 246–1800

**Wyoming**
United Student Aid Funds, Inc.
USA Group
11100 USA Parkway
Fishers, IN 46038
(800) 824-7044

**American Samoa, Guam, Northern
Mariana Islands, Federated States of
Micronesia, Marshall Islands, Republic
of Palau**
Hawaii Educational Loan Program
United Student Aid Funds, Inc.
1314 South King Street
Suite 861
Honolulu, HI 96814

**Puerto Rico**
Higher Education Assistance Corporation
Minillas Station
P.O. Box 42001
San Juan, PR 00940–2001
(809) 763–3535

**Virgin Islands**
Virgin Islands Joint Boards of Education
P.O. Box 11900
Charlottte Amalie
St. Thomas, VI 00801
(809) 774–4546

**United Student Aid Funds, Inc.**
USA Group
11100 USA Parkway
Fishers, IN 46038
(800) 824–7044 (in state)
(317) 849-6510

# Appendix I: List of Professional Associations

American Accounting Association (AAA)
5717 Bessie Drive
Sarasota, FL 34233-2399
(813) 921-7747

American Association for the
Advancement of Science
1333 H Street, NW
Washington, D.C. 20005
(202) 326-6400

American Association of Colleges for
Teacher Education
1 Dupont Circle, NW, Suite 610
Washington, D.C. 20036
(202) 293-2450

American Association of Colleges of
Nursing
1 Dupont Circle, NW
Suite 530
Washington, D.C. 20036
(202) 463-6930

American Association of University
Women
1111 16th Street, NW
Washington, D.C. 20036
(202) 785-7700

American Business Women's Association
(ABWA)
9100 Ward Parkway
P.O. Box 8728
Kansas City, MO 64114
(816) 361-6621

American Historical Association
400 A Street, SE
Washington, D.C. 20003
(202) 544-2422

American Indian Graduate Center (AIGC)
4520 Montgomery Boulevard, NE, Suite
   1-B
Albuquerque, NM 87109
(505) 881-4584

American Institute of Physics (AIP)
1 Physics Ellipse
College Park, MD 20740-3843
(301) 209-3100

American Management Association
(AMA)
135 West 50th Street
New York, NY 10020-1201
(212) 586-8100

American Marketing Association
250 South Wacker Drive, Suite 200
Chicago, IL 60606
(312) 648-0536

American Mathematical Society
P.O. Box 6248
Providence, RI 02940
(401) 455-4000

American Philosophical Association
University of Delaware
Newark, DE 19716
(320) 451-1112

American Political Science Association
(APSA)
1527 New Hampshire Avenue, NW
Washington, D.C. 20036
(202) 483-2512

American Psychological Association
750 1st Street, NE
Washington, D.C. 20002-4242
(202) 336-5500

American Sociological Association
1722 N Street, NW
Washington, D.C. 20036
(202) 833-3410

Association for Canadian Studies in the
United States
1 Dupont Circle, NW Suite 620
Washington, D.C. 20036
(202) 887-6375

Association for the Study of Higher
Education
Department of Educational Administration
Texas A&M University
College Station, TX 77843-4226
(409) 845-0393

Association of American Law Schools
(AALC)
1201 Connecticut Avenue, NW
Suite 800
Washington, D.C. 20036-2605
(202) 296-8851

Association of American Medical
Colleges (AAMC)
2450 N Street, NW
Washington, D.C. 20037
(202) 828-0400

Law School Admissions Council (LSAC)
P.O. Box 40
Newtown, PA 18940
(215) 968-1101

Mathematical Association of America
1529 18th Street, NW
Washington, D.C. 20036
(202) 387-5200

National Black MBA Association
(NBMBAA)
180 North Michigan Avenue, Suite 1515
Chicago, IL 60601
(312) 236-2622

National Hispanic Scholarship Fund
P.O. Box 728
Novato, CA 94948
(415) 892-9971

National Society of Public Accountants
(NPSA)
1010 North Fairfax Street
Alexandria, VA 22314-1574
(703) 549-6400

Native American Scholarship Fund
(NASF)
8200 Mountain Road, NE, No. 203
Albuquerque, NM 87110-7835
(505) 262-2351

# About the Author

Patricia McWade is Dean of Students Financial Services at Georgetown University. She currently serves as Vice Chairman of the Board of Directors of American Student Assistance, a student loan guarantee agency in Boston, is a member of the consortium on the Financing of Higher Education (COFHE) Financing Options Committee, and is a member of the national and regional financial aid associations. Dean McWade is a nationally recognized expert on the financing of both an undergraduate and graduate education. She brings to this book twenty-five years of experience helping students through the financial aid maze.

# Index

## Peterson's Guides to Graduate & Professional Programs 1997

*"A truly comprehensive resource. . . ."*
—Jules B. LaPidus, President, Council of Graduate Schools

*Match your field of interest to one of these Peterson's Guides! The most comprehensive* guides available, they provide detailed information on more than 1,500 colleges and universities offering over 31,000 master's, doctoral, and professional degree programs in more than 350 disciplines. Profiles in each book contain all essential information—entrance requirements, deadlines, and program contacts. Plus, in-depth descriptions from the individual institutions give more details. And, also in each Guide, The Graduate Adviser section discusses entrance exams, financial aid, accreditation, and more.

### Graduate and Professional Programs: An Overview (Book 1)
ISBN 651-0, 1, 412 pp., 8 1/2 x 11, $27.95 pb

### The Humanities, Arts, and Social Sciences (Book 2)
ISBN 652-9, 1,575 pp., 8 1/2 x 11, $37.95 pb

### The Biological Sciences (Book 3)
ISBN 653-7, 2,924 pp., 8 1/2 x 11, $44.95 pb

### The Physical Sciences, Mathematics, and Agricultural Sciences (Book 4)
ISBN 654-5, 1,038 pp., 8 1/2 x 11, $34.95 pb

### Engineering and Applied Sciences (Book 5)
ISBN 655-3, 1,714 pp., 8 1/2 x 11, $37.95 pb

### Business, Education, Health, Information Studies, Law, and Social Work (Book 6)
ISBN 656-1, 1,986 pp., 8 1/2 x 11, $27.95 pb

## How to Write a Winning Personal Statement for Graduate & Professional School
*Richard J. Stelzer*
This is *the* book to turn to for help in confronting one of the most challenging aspects of the admissions process—the personal statement. It offers perspectives of admissions officers, over 30 examples of successful statements, questions to ask yourself and others, tips on what not to include, and more.
ISBN 287-6, 150 pp., 6 x 9, $12.95 pb, 2nd edition

## The Ultimate Grad School Survival Guide
*Lesli Mitchell*
Takes you through the steps of finding the right university for graduate studies, taking the GREs, negotiating academic life, completing a degree, and even getting a job. Written by a current grad student, it's filled with helpful advice and insights from students and professors across the country.
ISBN 580-8, 256 pp., 7 x 9, $14.95 pb

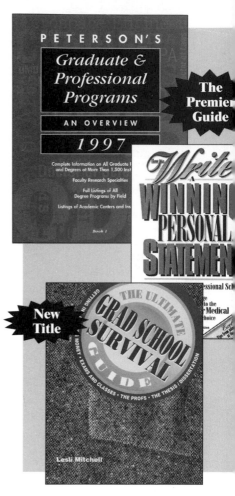

# Prepare for Graduate School Success with These Peterson's Titles

**The Premier Guide**

**New Title**

## Available at Fine Bookstores Near You

### Or Order Direct
Call: 800-338-3282   Fax: 609-243-9150

**Visit Peterson's Education Center on the Internet**
http://www.petersons.com

P Peterson's   P.O. Box 2123, Princeton, NJ 08520-4991

*ISBN prefix: 1-56*